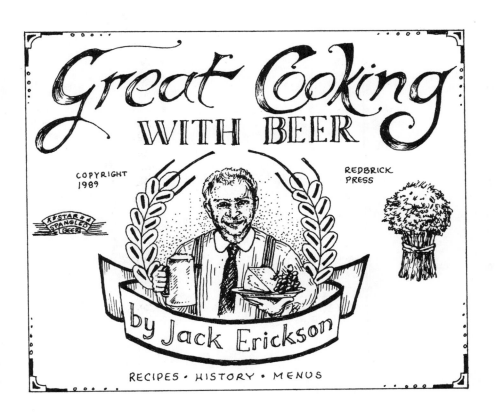

Great Cooking
WITH BEER

COPYRIGHT
1989

REDBRICK
PRESS

by Jack Erickson

RECIPES · HISTORY · MENUS

GREAT
COOKING
WITH
BEER

Jack Erickson

REDBRICK PRESS

RESTON, VIRGINIA

Published by:
RedBrick Press
P.O. Box 2184
Reston, VA 22090

ISBN 0-941397-01-7 (Paperback)
       0-941397-02-5 (Hardcover)

Library of Congress Catalog Card Number

88-092033

First Printing: August, 1989

Cover photo: Mark Borchelt
Cover location: Clyde's of Tysons, McLean, Virginia
Illustrations: Kate Sternberg

Printed on acid-free paper

Manufactured in the United States of America

10   9   8   7   6   5   4   3

In memory of Edna Erickson
who taught me
my first cooking lessons

Books by Jack Erickson
published by RedBrick Press

STAR SPANGLED BEER
A Guide to America's New Microbreweries and Brewpubs

T A B L E   O F   C O N T E N T S

Acknowledgements

What a job! Tasting the best beers brewed around the world, visiting breweries, cooking new dishes with specialty beers, inviting friends to sample the results, hosting beer dinners with restaurants, and meeting wonderful people along the way. All in the line of duty writing a beer cookbook.

The way I looked at it, with the growing popularity of specialty beers and the booming microbrewing phenomena, it was going to happen sooner or later — someone was going to write a contemporary beer cookbook. Little did I expect that it was going to be me.

Five years ago my cooking repertoire ran from barbecuing a few burgers on the grill to fixing Spanish omelets on the weekend and preparing the occasional dinner for friends. Not exactly the background one might expect for someone destined to write a cookbook.

So how did this book come to be? The original idea arose while I was promoting my book, "Star Spangled Beer," in California in the summer of 1987. Californians knew about microbreweries since the movement started there in the 1970s and they were familiar with imported beers and specialty beers brewed by the Anchor brewery in San Francisco, the Sierra Nevada brewery in Chico, and the West Coast brewpubs.

When I talked about specialty beers to Californians, a common response was something like, "You know what I like about these beers — they are great for cooking or having dinner with friends. Why don't you write a beer cookbook — these beers go great with food."

Great idea!

For the next year I researched the ales, porters, stouts and other specialty beers brewed around the world. I cooked with the beers and invited friends over to try the food. I would start with a blind beer tasting and then we would sit down for a three or four course dinner all cooked with beer.

The response was phenomenal — friends loved the beers and were surprised how good the food tasted. My thinking was, with my limited cooking expertise, if I could cook with these beers so could many others out there. I was convinced a cookbook featuring specialty beers would find an appreciate audience — particularly from readers wanting to know more about them and how they fit into the American cuisine.

So I did. This is the result. Hope you like it.

This book had the generous support and encouragement of a number of friends along the way. Mike Abraham of the Vienna Inn in Vienna, Virginia, was a loyal friend and supporter during all phases of the production of the book. John Cristea of Rehoboth Beach, Delaware, continued to give his encouragement and support.

Beth Schwartz of Manassas, Virginia, was invaluable as an assistant preparing many of the meals and recipes in the book. Her research, energy, patience, and commitment deserve special recognition. One day she'll write her own cookbook — I hope I can publish it.

Many of the ideas and refinements in this book were conceived at restaurants on the East Coast where I moderated beer tastings and dinners.

Don and Lynn Abram were early sponsors with beer dinners at The Calvert Grille, in Alexandria, Virginia.

Neil and Karen Elsohn of the Waters Edge Restaurant in Cape May, New Jersey, sponsored several beer dinners and gathered their favorite patrons from New Jersey, Pennsylvania, and Delaware.

Dane Wells of the Queen Victoria Inn in Cape May, a certified beer judge and connoisseur, provided keen insights and comments along the way.

Beverley Brockus was warm in her encouragement by featuring beer dinners at the Clyde's Restaurants in Washington, D.C.

Mike Harwood of The Dickens Inn in Philadelphia sponsored a dinner featuring British and Norwegian beers on a cold winter night.

Dan Kopman of the Young's Brewery, London, England, and the Real Beer Portfolio, opened many doors for me.

Hans J. Henschien of the Aass Brewery in Drammen, Norway, and the Real Beer Portfolio, was helpful in providing material for recipes.

Tom Ruddy and Allen Calford of Continental Breweries in Mississauga, Ontario, sponsored me at beer luncheons during their brewpub seminars.

Charles Finkel of Merchant du Vin importers in Seattle, Washington, George Saxton of Phoenix Imports in Baltimore, Maryland, the John

I. Haas Company of Yakima, Washington, and the North Dakota Barley Council provided valuable material for the book.

Kate Sternberg of Reston, Virginia, illustrated the beer bottles and title page.

Larry Washington of Manassas, Virginia, and Barbara Nealis of Sterling, Virginia, provided support during menu planning and recipe preparation.

The Association of Brewers, Boulder, Colorado, provided research material on brewpubs and beer styles.

Phil Katz of the Beer Institute in Washington, D.C., allowed frequent use of the institute's library and archives.

Ruth Logsdon designed the layout for the book, and Marlene Hochberg of Modern Typography provided typesetting.

Greg Noonan of the Vermont Pub and Brewery in Burlington, Vermont, read and corrected early portions of the manuscript.

Wendy Sizer of Warrenton, Virginia, Barbara Miller of New York, Nancy Weinberg, Irene Linton, and Cindy Drucker of Washington, D.C., were typically ready with a helpful suggestion or comment at the right time.

Marilyn McMorran continued to be as supportive as she always is as we cooked, ate, and sampled these wonderful beers and foods. Great fun, wasn't it Marilyn?

INTRODUCTION

A BEER COOKBOOK!

Something terribly exciting is happening in the world of beer — a renaissance in specialty brewing.

Creamy stouts from Ireland, hearty lagers from Germany and Czechoslovakia, exotic lambics from Belgium, Christmas beers from Britain and Switzerland, and other specialty beers from Japan, Australia, Mexico and Canada are flooding the American market and finding a thirsty and enthusiastic following.

Small breweries in the U.S. and Canada known as "microbreweries" are reintroducing beer styles — ales, porters, stouts, amber lagers, bock and Christmas beers — that hadn't been brewed in North America for over sixty years.

A wave of new "brewpub" restaurants, like the Commonwealth Brewery in Boston, the Devil Mountain Brewery in Walnut Creek, California, and the Blue Ridge Brewery in Charlottesville, Virginia, are reviving the wonderful American tradition of neighborhood tavern breweries that thrived from colonial days until Prohibition.

And even the big boys — Anheuser-Busch, Coors, Strohs, Miller and Heileman are test marketing specialty beers. Coors, the fifth largest brewery in the U.S. (1988 production: 16 million barrels) recently marketed nationwide two specialty beers: Winterfest, a Christmas beer, and Killian's Red.

This resurgent interest in specialty brewing has not escaped the attention of major media like Time Magazine, Newsweek, National Public Radio, NBC TV, and CBS News who are calling this trend a renaissance in brewing. Gourmet food and beer lovers haven't had it so good in years.

What to make of this . . . is it a new major trend among food conscious consumers or the revival of something more traditional?

THE OLDEST FERMENTED BEVERAGE IN HISTORY

Beer, of course, has been with us since before recorded history. Beer was carried aboard Noah's Ark, and the Pharoahs sacrificed thousands of barrels to the gods in annual offerings. Queen Elizabeth I drank a gallon of beer at breakfast, which was a custom of the day, and Henry VIII supervised the palace brewer at work.

The Pilgrims landed at Plymouth because they were running out of beer; they even had a recipe for beer syrup cooked with brown sugar to pour over pancakes. America's Founding Fathers — Benjamin Franklin, Samuel Adams, George Washington and Thomas Jefferson were all involved in brewing in the early days of the republic.

And virtually every European country has some national dish that uses beer as an ingredient — beer soup in Denmark, sausages boiled in beer in Germany, Carbonnade cooked in beer in Belgium, and the popular Welsh rarebit.

Cooking with beer is one of the most fascinating aspects of the renaissance in brewing. Not only are these specialty beers from every corner of the world wonderful beverages to drink by themselves or serve with food — they add a new dimension to cooking and menu planning for anyone willing to learn about them.

Irish stouts make a zesty marinade for roasts; amber lagers revive all-American standbys like hamburgers and chili; spicy ales go perfectly with steamed shrimp or barbecued chicken; and Belgian lambic beers brewed with cherries make a tantalizing ingredient in cakes and other desserts.

WHY A BEER COOKBOOK?

When John Porter was writing his book "All About Beer" in 1975, the state of the American beer industry had hit bottom. Major breweries had gobbled up smaller breweries, and the import beer market was a paltry 0.7%. The choice of beers available to the consumer was minimal. At such a low point, Potter was lamenting the lack of beer in American cuisine:

> ■ *For some unknown reason beer hasn't really caught on in the American kitchen. It may be that we simply haven't discovered all the things it can do for food, and for the cook! For example, it makes an admirable substitute for milk, water, chicken stock, beef broth, even wine, in any recipe you are now using. And you can use it for crisper batters, pancakes, soups, stews, pot roasts, and ultra-light souffles. The subtle flavor it adds to familiar foods is different enough to make them interesting, but not so pronounced as to make conservatives and children scream with surprise. Beer doesn't dominate the flavor of the dish; it somehow enhances it.*[1]

That situation didn't change in the subsequent decade, which saw the explosion in the popularity of import beers and the emergence of the microbreweries on the American market. To what do we owe that apparent void in appreciation for beer in cooking?

One conjecture has some sociological significance; for decades, beer has had the reputation of being a blue-collar drink, something that the guys put away after the late shift at the factory or at the bowling alley. Beer was considered so common that it belonged only in the taverns or in the cab of a pickup.

Another reason for the lack of appreciation has been the beer itself. The most popular American beer since the end of Prohibition is pale pilsner beer. After it is thinned with adjuncts such as corn and rice, pumped full of carbonation to create a temporary head, and pasteurized to give it a long shelf life, it loses much of the flavor and taste.

The social status of beer has changed dramatically since the early 1980s. Beer is no longer a drink for the "common" man — or woman. Beer has become more than "upscale," it has become trendy and popular. Style-conscious consumers today are seeking specialty beers and ales from Great Britain, Germany, Belgium, Italy, Switzerland, Norway, Japan, Australia, Canada, Mexico and other countries. Americans are not only enjoying beers from around the world, they're also discovering exotic styles that deserve more representation in American cuisine.

FEW BOOKS PUBLISHED ON BEER

When I started researching and writing "Great Cooking with Beer," I was puzzled that there was little written on the topic even though beer is the most popular alcoholic beverage in the world. I searched libraries and bookstores for beer cookbooks but could find few books and only an occasional magazine article. The Library of Congress lists fewer than a dozen beer cookbooks published in the last thirty years. That certainly was not what I expected regarding a basic food such as beer which, after all, has the same ingredients as bread — grain, yeast and water.

Late in 1987, however, I was encouraged when I found a book originally published in London in 1972 (now out of print) written by an English writer, Carole Fahy, called "Cooking with Beer." In her introduction Ms. Fahy wrote:

■   *When I started this book I was amazed at the number of my friends who had never heard of cooking with beer. Most of them knew of Welsh Rarebit; a few had heard of* Carbonnades Flamandes *and one, more enterprising, had actually eaten ham boiled in beer. But that was the extent of their knowledge.*

This is astonishing because we should be using our national drink to cook with as freely as we use wine. We should be doing as much to revolutionise [sic] cooking habits with beer as the French did with their national drink, because beer can have as superb an effect on the subtle flavor and conistency of our meals as any wine — and at a fraction of the cost.[2]

I was not the first to be puzzled at the lack of consumer awareness about cooking with beer and actually had a companion in spirit who had discovered these rewards years before I had. And although friends confessed that their experience cooking with beer was limited to an occasional beer batter or shrimp steamed in beer, they were enthusiastic about the venture and became willing recipe testers.

A New Approach:
LEARNING ABOUT BEER BEFORE COOKING WITH IT

"Great Cooking With Beer" is different from other information published on the subject.

First, the few books and magazine articles published in the past thirty years about cooking with beer offer sketchy information about beer as a basic food or explain why it is such an excellent ingredient for cooking. Most books have an introduction limited to a few paragraphs or pages about beer and then offer their recipes. They treat beer as if it were a generic product — like water or milk. They also discuss beers in such general terms that readers are left with the impression that beers are almost identical in ingredients and taste.

Anyone familiar with the vast differences between a light American lager, an Irish Stout, English ale, or Belgian lambic would be horrified at this cavalier attitude and lack of awareness about the range and complexity among beer styles.

Second, previous books and magazines also list beer in the recipes without recommending any specific style of beer. With more than thirty different beer styles to choose from, the reader had little information in previous books and articles to know which beer to use. Light lager? Pale ale? Porter? Double bock? Sweet stout?

A salad dressing prepared with pale ale would taste completely different if stout were used. The malts and hops used to brew pale ale (pale and caramel malt; Cascade, Fuggles and Golding hops) and stout (roasted barley and black patent malt; Clusters and Eroica hops) are very different. Any food prepared with them will likewise taste — and look — different.

Such a casual disregard for the range of beer styles would be comparable to a food writer listing "wine" in a recipe without indicating a red or white, sweet or dry. The difference, as it becomes obvious, is a critical one.

More Than A Collection Of Recipes

"Great Cooking with Beer" is more than a cookbook about beer; it is a celebration of beer as an historic and important beverage. Understanding the craft of brewing, the ingredients in beer, and the diversity in beer styles is only the beginning. To appreciate the tremendous changes going on in the world of beer, the reader should be aware of the creativity in brewing, marketing and serving specialty beers. This book is for readers who want to know more about cooking with beer than just recipes, ingredients and instructions.

Although the renaisssance in brewing begins in the brewery, it is being celebrated in restaurants, brewpubs, and homes where beer is featured as a beverage of moderation, good taste, and elegance. "Great Cooking With Beer" was written for the curious and adventurous reader looking for a new and exciting cuisine. To those readers, this challenge is issued:

Read this book. Shop for specialty beers. Taste them and serve them with your favorite dishes. Try a recipe and select the recommended beers to serve with a meal.

Then, when you are ready, plan a dinner party, invite friends, and tell them you have a "surprise" dinner — something they may never have tried before (it's probably fair to say that most people will not have tried these dishes with the exception of a beer batter, Welsh Rarebit or Carbonnade).

I guarantee you'll be pleased — not only with the new recipes, but with the introduction into the world of specialty beers featured in this book.

IT'S MORE THAN BEER — IT'S AN EXPERIENCE!

There's something to celebrate — beer isn't just "beer" anymore; it's a delightful beverage to share with family and friends who appreciate quality ingredients in cooking and a new experience in American cuisine. There is nothing "common" about beer anymore; this book is an acknowledgement that beer deserves more recognition as a product of diversity, creativity, and sophistication.

You're going to enjoy learning about beer and trying these recipes. I also hope you'll be as intrigued as I am by the rich historical and cultural traditions of beer from earliest recorded history through the rise of European civilizations and the first settlers in the New World to the present day.

Beer certainly is the most historic of all beverages. Until recently, it was also one of the least appreciated of all foods. That situation is undergoing a dramatic transformation as specialty beers become one of the most exciting features in American cuisine.   ■

CHAPTER ONE

THE RENAISSANCE OF BEER
OLDER THAN HISTORY

Dorset's famous chalk-cut hill figure stands 180 feet high and is claimed to be either the Celtic god 'Nodons' or a Romano-British representation of 'Hercules'. The Cerne Giant can be seen in all his glory on Giant Hill, Cerne Abbas north of Dorchester, and is celebrated in Eldridge Pope's "Cerne Giant Mead".

Dorset Characters N⁰ 1 in a series.

Eldridge, Pope & Co Ltd, Dorchester Brewery, Dorchester, Dorset.

Beer is older than recorded history and cooking with beer is probably one of the earliest methods of preparing food.

Anthropologists have found evidence of a fermented beverage made from wild grain at some of the first sites where early man settled. That malted beverage was an early form of beer.

Dr. Solomon Katz, professor of anthropology at the University of Pennsylvania, has conducted research on nutrition in early civilizations and has written that the discovery of beer probably was accidental when wild wheat or barley gathered to make gruel was fermented by naturally occurring yeast.[1]

Katz says that tribes of early man probably stored wild grain in damp caves where it became wet. When moist grain is exposed to air, it undergoes fermentation. When tribes of Neolithic man drank it, they were pleasantly surprised. It not only tasted good but gave them a feeling of mild euphoria.

The illustrations in this chapter are reproductions of beer coasters from the Eldridge Pope Brewery in Dorchester, England. They represent the cultural tradition of beer in the long and colorful history of the British Isles.

Picture, if you can, the excitement of such a discovery — Stone Age men and women sipping this sweet, malty beverage and being intrigued and surprised at its taste. It's not hard to imagine them beginning to feel the effects of the alcohol and getting a little dizzy. Soon they were slurping it down and feeling the pleasant effects as it warmed their insides and made them feel exhilarated. As soon as one batch of this fermented beverage was consumed, there was probably a frantic rush to prepare another.

Eureka! At last there was relief from the anxiety of daily foraging for food and struggling against bitter weather, ferocious animals and numbing hunger. The drudgery and monotony of Stone Age life was beginning to be a little more mellow.

FROM NOMADS TO FARMERS
— ALL BECAUSE OF BEER

Harry Paye

An artist's impression

T his celebrated Poole pirate was legendary in the 15th Century. Described in a contemporary Spanish chronicle as "this knight who scoured the seas . . . plundering all the Spanish and French vessels that he could meet with", 'Arripay' (as the Spanish spelt his name) often plundered in the more respectable office of Vice-Admiral of the Cinque Port Navy. The 'Old Harry' pub in Poole old town is named after him.

Dorset Characters №4 in a series.

Eldridge, Pope & Co Ltd, Dorchester Brewery, Dorchester, Dorset.

The discovery of brewing certainly ranks as one of *homo sapiens* epic achievements — as momentous as the harnessing of fire or the invention of the wheel. Once Neolithic tribes settled down to cultivate grains for brewing, they left nomadic life and became farmers. The transition from hunter-gatherer tribes to agricultural societies was made. Civilization as we know it was just around the corner — all because of the discovery of beer.[2]

These "beer drinking" tribes were also getting more nutrition from the fermentation of grains than the "non drinking" tribes. In the parlance of evolutionists, the "beer drinkers" were probably more fit to survive in the harsh environment of the Stone Age than the non-drinkers whose nutrition was deficient without the benefits of drinking the fermented grain.

Sociologists also say that all societies — even Neolithic man — have gone to great extremes to produce mood-altering substances such as alcohol or stimulating drugs for their socializing and salubrious effects.

The historical record of brewing in early civilizations is well-documented and universal. Even the world's oldest recipe — written on Sumerian tablets 5,000 years ago — is for beer.

Ramses III, king of Egypt in the 12th century B.C., poured thousands of gallons of beer on the altar annually as a royal sacrifice to the gods.

Egyptian hieroglyphics, the Code of Hammurabi, the Old Testament and the Magna Carta record the widespread commercialization of brewing. Along with bread, beer was a principal product of commerce and trade.

Archaeologists excavating in northeastern Syria in 1987 discovered clay tablets inscribed with cuneiform symbols dating from the 18th century B.C. More than two-thirds of the tablets were administrative records of financial transactions and distribution of the annual barley harvest. The beer brewed was for royalty and the tablets record that eighty liters of the "best quality" beer were provided for a dinner honoring "the man from Babylon."[3]

Beer was also a staple food in India, China, and South America. The Chinese were brewing a beer made from rice as early as 2300 B.C. The Incas in South America used corn to make their beer centuries before the Europeans arrived.

Finnish sagas, such as the Kalevala, and Norse legends rhapsodized about the marvelous effects of ale and recorded great drinking bouts during feasts which lasted for weeks.

MEDIEVAL EUROPE BECOMES INTERNATIONAL CENTER FOR BREWING

In medieval Europe ale was taxed and used for barter in international trade. Brewing in Germany was already advanced to such a state that in 1376 more than 1,000 registered brewers lived in Hamburg. In 1516 the elector of Bavaria decreed the famous Reinheitsgebot edict which required beer to be made from only three ingredients — malted barley, water and hops. Four hundred years later the Reinheitsgebot "purity law" is still in place in Germany and became the subject of a ruling by the European Economic Community in 1986.

In Europe the popularity of beer spread across all social classes from royalty to commoners. Early rulers demanded large amounts of beer at celebrations, weddings, feasts and banquets. England's Elizabeth I had a gallon of ale set aside for breakfast for her ladies-in-waiting and Henry IV ordered his brewer to make the royal ale without hops.

But beer was not just for royalty; commoners all over Britain visited alehouses daily and drank great quantities at a sitting. The modern

English pubs are directly descended from the coaching inns where weary travelers rested, ate, and drank freshly brewed ale on long journeys or religious crusades. These coaching inns and neighborhood public houses were the center for social and cultural life all over Britain.

BEER IN AMERICAN HISTORY

Beer was brewed in the New World even before Columbus arrived. On his fourth trip to America, Columbus found Indians drinking a form of beer that resembled English ale but was made with maize and pine tar.

The first settlers in Virginia even recruited brewers from London in 1609 because the colonists' first attempts at brewing were miserable failures. Farmers, artisans, fishermen could all work better when their beer was brewed by a professional and not an amateur; early records say that batches of "home-made" beer went bad and made settlers ill when they drank it. A journal kept aboard the Mayflower recorded that the Pilgrims landed in Massachusetts instead of Virginia because they "had run out of victuals, especially our beere."

THE BEVERAGE OF CHOICE FOR COLONISTS — ALE

Judge Jeffreys

A t his 'Bloody Assize' in Dorchester Judge Jeffreys tried the supporters of the Duke of Monmouth (illegitimate son of Charles II) after his unsuccessful attempt to secure the throne at the Battle of Sedgemoor. He condemned to death 292 of the 300 tried. They were hanged, drawn and quartered and their remains displayed in the towns and villages throughout Dorset.

Dorset Characters № 3 in a series.

Eldridge, Pope & Co Ltd, Dorchester Brewery, Dorchester, Dorset.

Ale brewing was an integral part of the culture and economic life in each of the original American colonies. Many farmers and tradesmen were involved with brewing, either by brewing at home for their own consumption or by supplying a local tavern. Ale was the most common beverage of all men, women and children in the colonies since water frequently was contaminated by humans or animals. The hops in ale was actually a preservative, since it killed small amounts of bacteria.

Founding Fathers George Washington, Samuel Adams, Benjamin Franklin, Thomas Jefferson and James Madison were all connected to brewing in some capacity when the nation's independence was declared in 1776. When Thomas Jefferson left the White House in 1809, he invited President James Madison to come to Monticello to observe his fall brewing.

FROM A CRAFT TO AN INDUSTRY

Waves of German immigrants brought to America a new style of beer called "lager" in the mid 1800s. Lager beer had been brewed earlier in the 19th century when a new yeast was discovered and beer was stored for long periods in cold caves (lager means to store in German).

When German brewers began brewing lager in America in the mid 1800s, they converted the nation from drinking English-style ales to German-style lagers. This conversion in taste coincided with the Industrial Revolution and the growth of cities such as New York, Pittsburgh, Milwaukee, and St. Louis, where northern European immigrants settled and German breweries thrived.

In the short space of 50 years, brewing in America evolved from a craft into a major industry. No longer were small breweries and tavern-owners brewing a few hundred barrels of ale for local consumption. By the end of the 19th century, legions of engineers, scientists and laborers worked in factories brewing millions of barrels of lager for industrial workers.

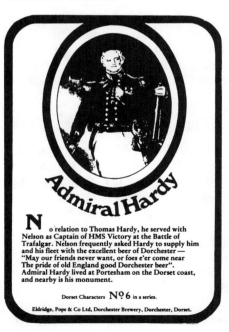

No relation to Thomas Hardy, he served with Nelson as Captain of HMS Victory at the Battle of Trafalgar. Nelson frequently asked Hardy to supply him and his fleet with the excellent beer of Dorchester — "May our friends never want, or foes e'er come near The pride of old England good Dorchester beer". Admiral Hardy lived at Portesham on the Dorset coast, and nearby is his monument.

Dorset Characters N⁰ 6 in a series.

Eldridge, Pope & Co Ltd, Dorchester Brewery, Dorchester, Dorset.

America even celebrated a Golden Age of Brewing in the 1870s, when brewery factories began producing a million barrels of beer per year. Brewing was one of the principal industries in America and employed thousands of brewers, coopers, laborers and truck drivers. In 1873, 4,131 breweries were operating — the largest number ever to exist in America.

At the Centennial Exposition of 1876 in Philadelphia, the major breweries erected a gigantic hall to celebrate the industry's achievements and growth in the nation's first century. Brewing belonged to the beer barons in the 19th century and not the tavern-brewers of the 18th century.

Brewing had even become such a profitable industry by the mid-19th century that three of the greatest wars this country ever fought — the Civil War, the Spanish-American conflict and World War I — were largely funded by taxes on breweries.

The decades from the Golden Age of Brewing to Prohibition in the 1920s were a time of great social and industrial upheavals in America. Like any other institution, brewing did not survive without disruption. Labor disputes forced work slowdowns, and several breweries closed after strikes and arson interfered with production.

More destructive in the long run, however, were the zealous prohibitionists whose wrath was aimed at the breweries and saloons around the country. In fifty years the romance and charm of brewing as a craft had been replaced by a labor-troubled industry that many considered greedy and corrupt.

Breweries had committed a near fatal sin — they had become ensnarled in national politics and rapidly changing social attitudes. During this tumultuous era the public relations skills of the brewers could be called only one thing — pitiful. The national image of the brewers was that they were in leagues with suspicious foreign powers (namely Germany) with the goal of weakening the national moral fiber with alcohol.

From being a beverage once praised by royalty and aristocrats, beer in America had become an evil substance, according to religious minorities and vocal Prohibitionists with powerful political connections. Their goal was to outlaw beer with a Constitutional amendment ratified by the states. By the turn of the century few politicians were brave enough to take up the cause of the brewers and defend their industry against the prohibitionists.

The Noble Experiment

When the 18th Amendment was ratified by the 36th state in January 1919, the goal of Prohibitionists was finally realized. On January 17, 1920, the Volstead Act went into effect, prohibiting the manufacturing, sale, transportation or consumption of any beverage exceeding 1/2 of 1% of alcohol. Across America nearly 2,000 breweries shut their doors — many never to open again.

From 1920 to 1933 the United States government embarked on a national mission to prohibit the sale and brewing of beer and other alcoholic beverages. It was a miserable failure; the law was violated from the moment it passed until the 23rd amendment repealing Prohibition went into effect April 7, 1933. Americans (and everyone else it seems) just love beer too much to obey even federal laws that interfere with what they consider a moral and legal right to consume alcohol.

During Prohibition, breweries were forced to make everything but beer — near beer, malt, bottled water, ice cream, ice, sodas, and cereals. Not every brewery obeyed the federal regulations and many — particularly in Chicago, New York and Philadelphia — brewed in violation of the law while corrupt state and federal officials looked the other way.

Roaring 20s gangsters Al Capone, "Bugs" Moran, and "Legs" Diamond found brewing a highly profitable venture. They controlled the supply of beer and other spirits to speakeasies where thirsty revelers paid triple costs for drinking the forbidden beverages.

Despite Prohibition, the U.S. still ranked sixth in beer production worldwide in 1926, brewing near-beer (.5% alcohol). Malt syrup production for homebrewing kept many breweries in business and grocery stores featured large displays of Blue Ribbon malt and Fleischmann's Yeast for enterprising "homebrewers." In 1926 and 1927, 888 million pounds of malt syrup was manufactured — enough to brew 7 million pints of beer![4]

MERGERS . . . CONSOLIDATIONS . . . CLOSURES

Many breweries that survived Prohibition simply could not compete after Repeal in 1933. After thirteen years of "non-production," many breweries were overwhelmed by the different economic environment when they started brewing again during the Depression. Antiquated equipment, a depressed economy, the strength of a few national breweries, and a blizzard of federal and state regulations were too much for many breweries, despite the pent-up thirst of the nation.

The competitive post-Prohibition environment favored the large, modern brewing factories that had grown into national manufacturers with several breweries around the country. With the economy of scale at their advantage, the larger breweries began a wave of consolidations, mergers and closures in the 1930s that became a feeding frenzy by the 1950s.

The once popular "hometown" beers were less attractive when nationally advertised and marketed beers such as Falstaff, Anheuser-Busch, Pabst, Schlitz, Rheingold, Schaefers, Ballantine, and Millers became available. Faced with stiff competition and declining markets, regional breweries began closing their doors; a colorful chapter in American history closed with them.

The mergers and consolidations saw another trend that disappointed beer lovers — a flood of homogeneous pale pilsener beers that all the national breweries produced. With national markets and advertising, the attitude of the national breweries seemed to be to brew a style of beer that would offend as few people as possible — a weak pale pilsener pumped up with artificial carbonation.

Virtually gone from the marketplace by 1960 were the ales, bock, porters, stout, festival and wheat beers that had once been part of the American beer scene. The major breweries also began adding adjunct grains like corn and rice to make the pale pilsener lighter, thinner and cheaper. The amount of hops used also declined with advertising boasting just "the kiss of hops" to indicate less bitterness and more sweetness.

A GROWING AWARENESS

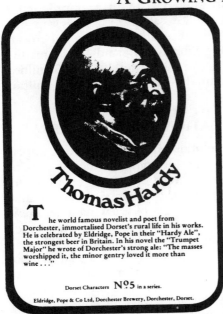

T he world famous novelist and poet from Dorchester, immortalised Dorset's rural life in his works. He is celebrated by Eldridge, Pope in their "Hardy Ale", the strongest beer in Britain. In his novel the "Trumpet Major" he wrote of Dorchester's strong ale: "The masses worshipped it, the minor gentry loved it more than wine . . ."

Dorset Characters N⁰5 in a series.

Eldridge, Pope & Co Ltd, Dorchester Brewery, Dorchester, Dorset.

With the advent of affordable commercial air travel after World War II, Americans began flying to Europe and other overseas destinations. Imagine their surprise when sampling the local cuisine in Germany, Italy, England, and Denmark and finding rich, flavorful beers so different from American pale pilsener beer. Imagine also their disappointment when they returned to the U.S. and had to go back to the same, boring pale pilsener beer.

A variety in beer styles became available in the American market from the same place smaller, cheaper cars came from — Europe and Asia. Heineken, Molson, Guinness, and Bass began developing a following when trend-setting food and beverage consumers began demanding more variety in their beer. If American breweries wouldn't produce for them, consumers would gladly turn to foreign breweries for diversity. Many of these imports merely copied the American pale pilsener style, but brewed with more hops to produce what many consider the "import" taste.

THE REVIVAL OF THE ANCHOR BREWERY

In 1965, in the midst of the beer "drought," a seemingly altruistic act by an idealistic graduate student in San Francisco became a watershed moment in the history of brewing in America. The idealist, washing-machine heir Fritz Maytag, was studying Asian civilizations at Stanford University when he heard that the nearly bankrupt Anchor Brewery in San Francisco was about to close.

Maytag visited the small brewery and fell in love with the idea of bringing it back to life. He bought it, began studying brewing, and revived the classic "steam beer" style which had been popular in California since Gold Rush Days. Although he probably didn't realize it, Maytag was firing the first shot in a revolution — a quiet brewing revolution in America.

A Tolpuddle Martyr

The Martyrs were six Dorset farm labourers, who in 1833 formed themselves into a union to resist a cut of one shilling in their weekly wage of nine shillings (45p). As a result they were arrested, tried, convicted under the Mutiny Act of 1797, and sentenced to serve 7 years in convict settlements in Australia. They were pardoned in 1836, and eventually released, after a national outcry. This case helped to establish the rights of trade unions in Britain.

Dorset Characters **No. 2** in a series.

Eldridge, Pope & Co Ltd, Dorchester Brewery, Dorchester, Dorset.

Then, in 1977, another California pioneer, Jack McAuliffe, opened the New Albion Brewery in Sonoma in the heart of the wine country. McAuliffe had been in the Navy in Scotland and fell in love with English and Scottish ales. When he returned to the U.S., he began homebrewing to produce specialty beers shunned by American beer factories.

It didn't take long for McAuliffe's friends to convince him he should go commercial and open a small brewery to sell his beer. From McAuliffe's shed on the outskirts of Sonoma, America's first "microbrewery" was born out of old dairy equipment and junk yard salvage.

McAuliffe was part of a group of former servicemen and students who, upon their return to the U.S., turned a homebrewing hobby into a microbrewing business in the late 1970s and early 1980s. Eschewing the weak pale pilsener style, these microbrewing pioneers enthusiastically brewed distinctive ales, porters and stouts they had discovered overseas.

It wasn't long before other entrepreneurs inspired by Maytag and McAuliffe began having similar dreams of brewing specialty beers. By the early 1980s, microbreweries and "brewpubs" (restaurants where beer is brewed on the premises) had opened in New York, Colorado, Washington, Oregon.

The original microbrewers, with the exception of Fritz Maytag, were a group of eccentrics who brewed beer not too much different from homebrew. The next generation of microbrewers, however, were entrepreneurs who saw an opportunity to brew specialty beers — amber lagers, ales, porters, stouts and seasonal beers — that could survive in a competitive marketplace alongside Anheuser-Busch, Coors, Millers, Heineken, Molson and Becks.

REVIVAL OF CRAFT BREWING

Since Maytag purchased the Anchor Brewery in 1965 and McAuliffe opened the New Albion brewery in 1977, more than 200 microbreweries and brewpubs have opened in the United States and Canada. The movement has captured the imagination of the public and earned the respect and appreciation of millions of beer lovers in North America.

In a little over a decade the microbrewing movement has revived the art of small-scale craft brewing and developed an appreciation for fine beer in North America. Although the volume of beer they brew is relatively small (.1% of national production in 1988), the microbreweries have opened up a market for specialty beers brewed locally and in many styles.

Michael Jackson, the preeminent British beer writer, has noted this renaissance in his "Pocket Guide To Beer":

■   *There is an international wave of serious interest in Beer, from Italy (where it is the most chic of drinks), through Germany and Belgium (where specialty styles are in ever-greater demand) to Britain (first came the "real ale" renaissance; now the surge of "foreign" lagers) and to the United States (where imported beers arrive in bewildering profusion). In all of these countries, there has also been in recent years a blessing of new, tiny boutiques or micro breweries, often producing specialty styles of beer.*[5]

The major news media are also discovering that beer is a topic the public wants to know more about. Stories about microbrewery openings and beer tastings have been appearing regularly in national magazines and newspapers like the Washington Post, New York Times, Boston Globe, Esquire, Travel & Leisure and Glamour. Stories about beer don't appear only on the business page anymore — they've moved to the home, food, and style sections where lifestyle trends are chronicled.

The interest in specialty beers and microbreweries also has spawned a cottage industry of publications reporting on them. Four magazines and one newsletter are published in the West alone: "New Brewer" and "Zymurgy" (Association of Brewers, Boulder, Colorado), "All About Beer" (Bosak Publishing, Oceanside, California), "American Brewer" (Hayward, California), and "California Celebrator" (Pleasanton, California).

The "World Beer Review" newsletter published in South Carolina (WBR Publications, Clemson), and a new magazine, "The World of Beer," (Tuttopress Editrice, Milan and Dallas) take a more worldly view, as their titles indicate. The English ale society Campaign for Real Ale (CAMRA) publication, "What's Brewing," (St. Albans, Hertfordshire) remains the Bible for reporting news from the British Isles on small breweries and pubs, and a Canadian publication, "Northern Brewer" (Toronto, Ontario), covers the burgeoning microbreweries north of the border.

A NATIONWIDE RENAISSANCE OF BEER

No one knows how far this renaissance in specialty beers will go, but if the growth of the domestic wine industry is any indication, the future is virtually unlimited. Several factors would indicate that this renaissance is potentially far-reaching and should last into the next century:

1) Beer is America's favorite alcoholic beverage;
2) Beer is a drink of "moderation" at a time of growing concern for health and safety;
3) The microbrewing and brewpub revolution sweeping across the country has attracted legions of young and affluent beer lovers;
4) A desire by food and beverage conscious consumers to want variety and quality in all styles of food;
5) A growing appreciation for the heritage of brewing in American history.

While wine is considered a drink of the middle and upper class, the popularity of beer reaches all classes. Fritz Maytag of the Anchor Brewery also owns a California vineyard and is a philosopher about the popularity of both beer and wine.

"When I meet someone and tell them I am a brewer," Maytag said in an interview, "they have a personal story to tell me about beer — someone in their family who brewed beer or their favorite beer.

"But if I mention I have a vineyard people change the subject. They feel intimidated discussing wine because of its "snobbish" image. Beer, on the other hand, is a common man's drink and anybody can talk about beer with some authority because they've been drinking it since they were teenagers. Beer is more universal than wine."

If history is any indication, beer is going to be with us for a long time. A renaissance means that specialty beers — whether brewed in America or overseas — are going to awaken millions to the heritage of beer and its place in American cuisine.

Samuel Adams Double Bock
Boston Beer Company
Boston, Massachusetts

CHAPTER TWO

BEER IS A FOOD!

Beer is an excellent supplement to cuisine because it is refreshing and cleansing to the palate. Its ingredients stimulate the taste buds and enhance the gustatory experience.

Before starting to cook with beer, let's learn a little about beer, how it is brewed, its ingredients and why those ingredients are such an excellent complement to cooking. First of all, let's get clear what beer is and what it's not.

Beer is a food, pure and simple. With the same ingredients as bread — water, yeast, and grain (plus hops added for aroma and bitterness) — it is such a universal staple that it can be served with virtually any food group.

Beer is a large class of fermented malt beverages with a variety of styles, flavors, tastes and aromas.

Beer is nutritious, with healthful ingredients including niacin, riboflavin and calcium.

Beer is a moderately alcoholic beverage (3.5-4.5% alcohol by weight for most beers) that can be used in cooking many dishes, from appetizers and salads through main courses and desserts. Beer color can range from pale straw, golden, and amber to copper, nut-brown, reddish-brown and coal-black.

Beer flavors run the spectrum from weak, bland and fizzy to sweet, bitter and tart.

Beer is NOT alcoholic when used in cooking. As soon as it is heated to approximately 173° F (78° C) the alcohol evaporates, leaving the other ingredients — malted barley, hops and yeast — to flavor the food.

BEER IS MORE THAN PILSENER

Beer is NOT limited to the pale-yellow, pilsener style familiar to most Americans by slick advertising in newspapers, magazines, billboards and television.

Despite the fact that the fizzy, slightly sweet pilsener-style lager is the most popular beer in the world, to many beer lovers it is boring and tasteless. Advertising claims of "beechwood aging," "firebrewed," "tastes great . . . less filling," and "brewed the American Way," would lead consumers to believe that these are different beers. They're not; they're all the same pale-pilsener beers.

Pale-pilsener beers may be adequate for boiling shrimp and making batter, but they would enhance few other meals requiring flavoring ingredients. The major breweries' pilsener beers are brewed with less than 100% malted barley and a modest amount of hops — the two ingredients that make beer distinctive in cooking. If you want quality results from cooking with beer, you need beers with abundant quantities of malted barley and hops.

There are, fortunately, many other styles of beer. In this diversity comes the creative aspect of cooking and serving beer with all sorts of foods.

INGREDIENTS IN BEER

MALTED BARLEY

Barley used in brewing is grown around the world but chiefly in the American Midwest and Europe. Two-row barley is the most common grain used for brewing; six-row barley is also used because it is more plentiful and less expensive, but it produces less flavor. The two-row and six-row refers to the number of rows of grain on the stalk. Two-row barley contains less protein and malts more easily making it the more desirable variety for brewing.

Protein in barley is not desired in brewing since it makes the grain difficult to malt and ferment. For maximum sugar content, a barley variety rich in carbohydrates is preferable, since fermentable sugars end up being converted into alcohol during fermentation.

Malting barley growing on a North Dakota farm.

ADJUNCT GRAINS

Corn and rice are commonly used by breweries as adjunct grains in brewing. When these ingredients are mashed, boiled and fermented, the beer they produce is light, thin, and pale. Adjunct grains are cheaper, and their use by the industrial breweries has increased significantly over the last few years. A cheap domestic beer may have only about 60% malted barley with corn or rice in the form of syrup or flakes accounting for the remaining 40% of the grain.

Germany, Switzerland and Norway still brew according to the Reinheitsgebot, which permits only malted barley in brewing. Wheat is also used to brew specialty beers, a tradition that survives from old Europe. Weiss (wheat) beer has a spritzy, effervescence, lactic taste that makes it a refreshing summertime drink that is frequently served with a twist of lemon.

HOPS

A poet would describe hops as the perfume of beer — the delicate bouquet that tantalizes the olfactory senses. Hops also provide the distinctive bitter taste that lingers on the palate as a memorable, pleasurable effect. Without hops, beer would taste malty, sweet and cloying.

Hops are a climbing vine in the Cannabis family that grows like wild grapes. The female flower of the hop is the only part of the plant desired. The hop flower is actually a cone (strobile) consisting of over-lapping petals (bracteoles). Seeds at the base of the bracteole and yellow glands in the cone contain the oils and resin used in brewing.

Hops are used for taste and aroma in beer. A brewer may use two different types of hops: bittering hops for the bitter taste; aromatic hops for the bouquet.

In early brewing days (prior to pasteurization), hops acted as a pre-servative since beer was prone to spoilage from bacteria in the air and wild yeast.

A field of hops in Washington's Yakima Valley.

We can thank early brewers for the trial-and-error discovery of hops as a critical ingredient in beer. Early brewers — possibly as far back as ancient Rome and Greece — may have used hops in brewing. Other herbs like juniper berries, coriander and bay leaves were also used by early brewers to impart flavor and bitterness to ales. Hops were also placed in "hop pillows" because of their soporific effect; King George III used hop pillows to calm his nerves and help him sleep.

Brewing hops include many European and American varieties. They are chosen for their bitterness and aromatic properties. Hops with a high alpha acid content are a "bittering" hop. Some common varieties include:

AROMATIC HOPS

Hallertauer Mittelfruh — old German variety, sparsely grown in U.S, popular in lighter lagers;

Tettnanger — old German variety, sparsely grown in U.S.;

Fuggle — originally from England, common in U.S. since 1900, widely used variety in strong ales;

Willamette — developed in Oregon in late 1970s;

Cascade — a relatively new American variety, used extensively by many American brewers today; and

Perle — recently developed German strain; high alpha acid content.

MATURE HOP-CONE & SEEDED BRACTEOLE

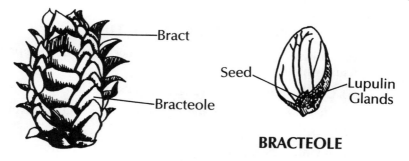

Bract

Bracteole

Seed

Lupulin Glands

BRACTEOLE

CONE   *Parts of a female hop cone.*

BITTERING HOPS
(high alpha acid content)

Chinook — developed in Washington in 1985;

Cluster — oldest variety in the U.S., common in pale pilseners;

Galena — developed in Idaho in late 1970s;

Eroica — developed in Idaho in 1980;

Nugget — developed in Oregon in 1982;

Olympic — developed in Washington and released in 1984.

Female hop flowers.

EUROPEAN HOP VARIETIES

Bullion — bittering hop used in stouts and beers brewed long periods, usually blended with other hops;

Brewer's Gold — English hop variety, popular in ales;

Northern Brewer — harsh bittering hop, falling out of favor with brewers;

East Kent Goldings — developed in early 19th century in Kent, England, commonly used in light ales;

Saaz — grown in Czechoslovakia, popular among German brewers for lager beers.

(Information courtesy of John I. Haas, Inc; 1615 L Street, N.W., Washington, D.C. "Hop Varieties, U.S. Grown")

YEAST

If there is anything approaching the "brewers' jewels," it is yeast which converts sugar to alcohol during fermentation. Yeast is literally the key that yields the subtleties and complexities of beer's taste and flavor during fermentation. Before they completely understood the role of yeast in brewing, early brewers used to call the mysterious organism "God is good," no doubt because of the wonderful product of fermentation.

Although Anton Van Leeuwenhoek first isolated yeast under the microscope in 1680, it took another 200 years and the studies of Louis Pasteur on beer to understand the critical role it played in fermentation.

The Norwegian chemist Emil Hansen of the Carlsberg Brewery is credited with identifying many strains of yeast including the sugar-reducing, alcohol-producing *saccharomyces*. Hansen isolated a yeast strain (*saccharomyces carlsbergensis*) used in brewing bottom-fermented lager beers.

To the chemist, yeast is *saccharomyces*, with specific varieties used for different styles of beer. *Saccharomyces carlsbergensis* is used to ferment "bottom-fermenting" lager beers (bottom-fermenting means the yeast falls to the bottom of the vessel after fermentation). *Saccharomyces cerevisiae* is used for brewing ales which are "top-fermenting" (the yeast rises to the top during fermentation). *S. cerevisiae* is also used for baking bread.

Under the microscope, yeast appears as random clumps of dough. The microorganism behaves erratically and can become contaminated if wild yeast infect the culture. Breweries raise yeast in their laboratories but will also reuse it as long as it is pure. If a yeast behaves erratically, a brewery may have to obtain yeast from another brewery or laboratory specializing in brewing yeast.

A pure strain of high quality yeast and average ingredients can produce a good beer; poor yeast, even used with high-quality malt and hops, will produce an inferior beer.

WATER

Contrary to barrages of advertising and well-intentioned public relations efforts, there is nothing magical or mystical about water in brewing. City water from an industrial urban center can actually be as good for brewing beer as the water from a glacial-fed mountain lake. A brewer looks for water that is slightly "hard," which means it contains calcium sulfate or other salts dissolved in the water.

English ales brewed at Burton-on-Trent are famous because the water has a relatively large amount of gypsum (calcium sulfate), which makes the water "hard." Soft water, on the other hand, lacks calcium. The calcium content in hard water helps separate the husks from the malt and produces a clear beer.

Early breweries boasted that the uniqueness of their water was the secret to their fine beer. But today most breweries draw their water from the city water supply and may make minor chemical adjustments before brewing.

THE BREWING PROCESS

Brewing is at once a simple yet complex procedure. Reduced to its simplest steps, barley is steeped in warm water until the grain begins to germinate or sprout. After germination, the grain is dried; this is malt.

The malt is milled and "mashed" into hot water to extract fermentable sugars before the liquid is boiled along with hops. After cooling yeast is added to begin fermentation. The beer is stored in chilling tanks after fermentation until ready for kegging or bottling.

MALTING

Prior to malting, barley is stored in dark bins to prepare it for the vigorous germination process. The first step in germination is washing the grain to prepare the barley for absorbing warm water. The grain occasionally will be aerated and rewashed to prevent suffocation.

After bathing the barley, the water is removed to let germination begin. Proper temperature, humidity and aeration are monitored to ensure optimum conditions. Germination takes approximately 36 hours and occurs when the grain has absorbed about 45% of its weight in water.

Germination produces heat, which must be controlled. Ideal germination temperature is between 52-64° F (12-18° C). Below this temperature germination will be hampered; above this temperature, undesirable chemical reactions can occur. In today's modern breweries, malting is monitored by computers, hydrometers, and thermometers. The key is to stop germination when the maximum starch conversion has taken place and before tiny shoots begin consuming the sugar

MASHING

When germination is complete, the barley malt is heated in a kiln. The color and taste of beer are a function of this roasting process. The heat kills the sprouts which stops germination. Before kilning, the grain may consist of as much as 45% water. This water must be reduced to 4% before the grain can be stored, since it may be months before the grain is shipped to a brewery.

The temperature of the kiln can vary from 140° to 450° F depending upon the desired color and taste of the malt. Pale-colored beers come from lightly heated barley; dark-colored beer is brewed with malt that has been roasted like coffee.

Lower temperatures (175° F) will produce pale malts for brewing golden-colored ales and lagers. The barley is heated but not "cooked;"

germination is stopped but enzymes are not killed. Beer brewed from pale malts tends to be crisp and clean tasting.

Medium temperatures (230° F) kill the embryo and some enzymes in the barley and produce a slightly nutty taste.

Higher temperatures (250° F) and moist barley produce crystal or caramel malt from the fermentable sugars that are caramelized. Bock beers and amber lagers brewed with caramel malt taste sweet and nutty.

The highest temperatures (450° F) kill the enzymes and roast the grains. Roasted malts are used for brewing dark porters and black-as-licorice stouts. Darker beers generally have a mocha or chocolatey taste.

Some specialty beers are a blend of pale, amber, crystal, and roasted malts which produce a characteristically complex and rich taste.

BREWING

Malted barley and other grains are added to a mash tun vessel where hot water is introduced. The resulting mash converts the starches into fermentable sugars. Two brewing methods are infusion, in one vessel for one or two hours, and decoction, where portions of mash are moved to a kettle then returned to the mash tun until the temperature reaches approximately 170° F.

The resulting sweet, hot "wort" is piped into a brewkettle and boiled for one to three hours. Hops are added to the boiling mixture in pellets, extract oils, or whole. After boiling, the hops are removed and the wort is cooled before passing to the fermentation vessel where yeast is added.

FERMENTATION

Primary fermentation takes place in temperature-controlled vessels. Ales are top-fermented with yeast (*saccharomyces cereviseae*) that works at warmer temperatures (50-65° F). During fermentation, the yeast rises to the top where it is skimmed and used again.

Ales ferment for about a week and are passed on to storage vessels for a few days where priming sugar may be added to stimulate a secondary fermentation. Natural carbonation during this secondary fermentation produces a rocky head when the beer is tapped and poured.

Lager is fermented by "bottom-fermented" yeast (*saccharomyces carls-bergensis*) at cooler temperatures (40-55° F). After fermentation, lager yeast falls to the bottom where it is collected and used again.

The word lager comes from the German word "to store" which is what brewers did to their beer to produce the clean, clear taste distinctive to the lager style. German brewers of the early 19th century lagered their beer for months in Bavarian ice caves in the alps or in underground caverns.

PASTEURIZATION

After beer is kegged or bottled, it frequently undergoes pasteurization — heating in warm water baths — to kill yeast and stop fermentation. Depending upon the point of view, pasteurization can be a blessing or a curse. The process stabilizes the beer and prevents spoilage — a common problem before Louis Pasteur's experiments with beer.

Pasteurization, however, also disrupts the natural carbonation of fermentation. Connoisseurs affirm that pasteurization eliminates the subtle flavor, taste, and aroma of well-brewed beer.

The finished product — Coor's specialty lager, Killian's Red.

A CHEMICAL ANALYSIS OF BEER

A chemical analysis of beer reveals that it consists of about 92% water, approximately 3 to 4% alcohol, and about 4% solids, carbohydrates, extracts and protein. These ingredients include albumin, dextrin, organic compounds, minerals and sugar. Beer contains many important ingredients that enhance health — calcium, niacin, phosphorus, riboflavin.

The average 12 oz. beer contains 140 calories (as compared to 80 calories for 1¼ oz. of Scotch, 142 calories for 2 oz. of gin, 230 calories for 12 oz. glass of milk, or 170 calories for soft drink). A 12 oz. beer also contains:

Protein	1.6 grams
Fat	0.0 grams
Carbohydrates	15.9 grams
Water	92%
Ethyl Alcohol	3.8%
Solids & Extracts	4.2%
Calcium	15 mg
Phosphorus	93 mg
B1 Thiamine	18.7 mgm
B2 Riboflavin	40-100 mgm
B6 Pyridoxin	185 mgm
Niacin	2200-3700 mgm
Pantothenate	185-375 mgm

Although the human taste buds can identify only four basic tastes (sour, sweet, bitter, salty), research by flavor chemists has identified more than 850 flavor compounds in beer, including the substances dimetyl sulfide, isohumulone, isoamyl acetate, ethyl hexanoante, ethanol, diacetyl, fusel alcohols and acetic, butyric, isovaleric and octanoic acid.

The alcohol in beer, ethanol, once was considered tasteless; recent research, however, indicates it has a "warm and pleasant flavor" when purified.

Hops contribute isohumulone (the dominant bitter flavor in beer), spicy and floral aromatic oils, fusel alcohol and carbon dioxide. Hops contain humulone, which changes chemically to isohumulone when hops are boiled in the brewkettle.

Isoamyl acetate, a flavor component in bananas, and ethyl hexanoate, a flavor component in apples, appear in fermentation and are referred to as "esters" (esters are formed when alcohol and acid occur in fermentation).

Diacetyl and pentanedione produce buttery flavors; polyphenols are "tea-like;" and isovaleric acid, a derivative of hops, tastes "cheesy;" amino acids provide body and peptides provide body and foam; isohumulones are "bitter." Although hundreds of other compounds have been identified, their tastes have not been defined.

THE BREWERS WORK OF ART — AND SCIENCE

The beer that arrives at your table or home is the result of centuries of the brewers' science and art. No simple beverage, it represents the determination of what the brewer believed you would find desirable whether it be a thirst-quenching lager, a spicy ale, or sipping porter. Regardless of the beer style you selected, there is a food that would be complemented by its flavor and taste.

All the ingredients in beer — malted barley, hops, water and yeast — enhance the taste of food. Malted barley lends body and flavor; hops are similar to spice; yeast (in small quantities) can add a hint of tartness.

When used as a marinade, beer tenderizes and moistens meat and imparts a spicy tang from the hops. In basting, beer produces a malty brown glaze with a hint of spice.

Much as people started switching from "hard liquor" to wine a few years ago in the interest of health and safety, they have already started switching from wine to lower-alcohol beers. That trend will likely continue when more people choose moderation in their consumption of alcohol and discover the many specialty beers that simply weren't available ten years ago.

Restaurant patrons have already discover brewpubs and their wonderful beers. The more curious they become about specialty beers the more likely they are to seek them out when they travel, plan dinner menus, attend beer tastings or start reading about them. Along the way the more adventurous will try cooking with specialty beers and treating dinner guests with several of them. Everybody will be delighted with the results.

The characteristics that beer adds to food vary with the variety in the ingredients; a pale ale or pilsener beer brewed with pale malt will add a light malty flavor to meat and fish dishes; a hearty stout or porter brewed with darker, roasted malts will add body and character to red meats and stews; a dessert or salad using a lambic fermentation beer will have a spicy, winey flavor.

There is such a great variety in specialty beers that almost any dish can have beer as an ingredient to bring out a special flavor or taste. The way to learn about these tastes is to experiment with specialty beers to discover which ones complement your style of cooking.

Which beer to choose? Let's take a look at the selection.

Sheaf Stout
Carleton & United Breweries
Sydney, Australia

CHAPTER THREE

THE WIDE WORLD OF BEER

T he delight of cooking with beer is the variety of beers from which to choose. These choices range from light pilsner beers brewed by most North American breweries to the spicy English ales, smoky Irish Stouts, full-bodied European lagers and exotic Belgian lambic-style ales. Within those broad ranges are a world of distinctive tastes to please any connoisseur and complement whatever style of cooking you choose.

Such a claim might seem a bit of a mystery to someone whose only experience with beer is the bland pale pilsener brewed by most breweries around the world. One of the exciting benefits of learning to cook with beer is discovering the bounty of wonderful and distinctive beers brewed by true craftsmen.

A BREWER AS CRAFTSMAN

To appreciate the craft of brewing one might want to consider the person responsible for producing specialty beers. A brewer undergoes years of education and training at an institute or university to learn the complex chemistry of brewing.

Consider, for example, the simple act of boiling the sweet wort and adding hops. Some decisions the brewer must make include:

How long should the boil last?

What variety of hops should be added and how much?

At what point in the boiling process should the hops be added?

What is the proper amount of hops to add at the beginning of the boil?

To what temperature should the wort be lowered when the yeast is pitched to start fermentation?

These are just a few of the many critical decisions a brewer must make during the brewing process which last for months from the time barley is malted and milled until the finished beer is removed from storage tanks for bottling or kegging.

Beer is a fragile and highly perishable commodity, and its production must be carefully monitored at all steps from the time the grain and hops are in the field to the brewery where the ingredients undergo the complex fermentation process.

A brewer must have all the skills of an artist, baker, engineer, chemist, and gourmand as he strives to create a distinctive beer worthy of the approval of his exacting peers and a demanding public. Like any artist, a brewer wants to be appreciated for creating a work of merit and distinction.

A fine, well-brewed beer is a work of art just as much as a painting or a piano concerto. They all require an enormous amount of time, knowledge, dedication, experimentation, creativity, and inspiration.

TYPES OF BEER

There are two main beer types — lager and ale — determined by the yeast and method of fermentation.

Ale is the first beer ever brewed and the only beer type known until the 19th century when science enabled brewers to examine the yeast responsible for fermenting the rich, sweet wort. Once the properties and characteristics of yeast were studied, variations in yeast strains could be produced in the laboratory. That experimentation lead to the discovery of different yeast, and, in particular, the strain which could produce the second major type of beer — lager. That discovery did not come until the 1840s.

Within these two main categories of beer are some 30 different styles of beer whose flavor and strengths can vary depending upon the variety of malts and hops used, the amount of malt per barrel, the temperature of the mash, the length of fermentation, the length of lagering or storing and a myriad of other factors known only to the brewmaster.

ALE STYLES

Ale yeast (*saccharomyces cerevisae*) works at relatively warm temperatures (55-65° F) and rises to the top of the vessel when fermentation is completed. Ales are called top-fermenting beers and are generally spicier, fruitier and more complex because of the yeast and fermentation temperature. Ales typically should be drunk warmer (55-60° F) to appreciate their features.

(Beers listed as representative of a particular style were selected because of their general availability in the North America market.)

Main styles of ale include:

TRAPPIST or ABBEY ALE — fruity, complex, full-bodied, with a distinctive hop bouquet. Most abbey-style ales are bottle conditioned which allows fermentation to continue after the beer leaves the brewery.

Abbey ales have rich and varied tastes — port-like, chocolatey, bitter-orange, or mildly nutty. There are many abbey-style ales but only five Belgian and one Netherlands monasteries continue to brew these wonderful beers. The monastery breweries have been working for centuries to produce distinctive, exotic beers that are highly regarded among connoisseurs.

Orval Trappist Ale *(Belgium)*
Chimay *(Belgium)*
St. Sixtus *(Belgium)*
Rochefort *(Belgium)*

BARLEY WINE — a strong ale, generally more than 5% alcohol by weight. The name originated over 100 years ago in England when brewers began brewing ales with strength closer to fruit wines. The name now is required by state laws in California and other jurisdictions to identify stronger beers. Best served as after-dinner drink or with dessert; excellent for cooking, especially in sweet Christmas cakes.

Domestics
Sierra Nevada Bigfoot Barley Wine *(California)*
Anchor Old Foghorn Barley Wine *(California)*

Imports
Young's Old Nick Barley Wine *(England)*

BROWN ALE — Brewed with darker malts to produce sweet or slightly nutty taste, possibly with a hint of honey or spice. Belgian brown ales can range from tart and tangy to sweet and heavy. The strength of brown ales range from weaker English mild ales to "old ale" or "winter warmer" style holiday beers.

> **Samuel Smith Nut Brown Ale** *(England)*
> **Gouden Carolus** *(Belgium)*
> **Palm Ale** *(Belgium)*
> **Liefmans Goudenband** *(Belgium)*
> **Newcastle Brown Ale** *(England)*

IMPERIAL STOUT — strong, robust stout first brewed in England for Romanov Czars in St. Petersburg in the 19th century. High alcohol content (9-10% by weight).

Domestics
Grant's Russian Imperial Stout *(Yakima)*

Imports
Samuel Smith's Imperial Stout *(England)*
Courage Imperial Russian Stout *(England)*

The Samuel Smith Brewery of Yorkshire, England,
produces a popular line of specialty ales, porters and stouts:
Pale Ale, Taddy Porter, Nut Brown Ale, and Oatmeal Stout.

Boulder Pale Ale, Boulder, Colorado   *Pacific Crest Ale, Kalama, Washington*

PALE ALE — the most prolific ale style ranging from very sweet to very bitter; most have a good balance of hops and malt. The most popular style of beer in Britain including hundreds of draught "bitters," numerous bottled ales, India Pale Ales, light ales, and strong pale ales.

Many North American microbreweries are finding success in brewing pale ales for regional markets. By their example, they are showing the brewing community that a style that had virtually disappeared in Canada and America can be revived profitably.

Domestics

Anchor Liberty Ale (*California*)
Sierra Nevada Pale Ale (*California*)
Boulder Pale Ale (*Colorado*)
Kessler Pale Ale (*Montana*)
Hart Pyramid Ale (*Washington*)
Red Hook Extra Special Bitter (*Washington*)
Harpoon Ale (*Massachusetts*)
Gearys Pale Ale (*Maine*)
Catamount Gold (*Vermont*)
Dock Street (*Pennsylvania*)

Imports

Samuel Smith's Old Brewery Pale Ale *(England)*
Bass Pale Ale *(England)*
Young's Special London Ale *(England)*
Fullers Extra Special Bitter *(England)*
John Courage *(England)*
Royal Oak *(England)*
Whitbread *(England)*
Cooper's Real Ale *(Australia)*

PORTER — heavier, rich dark ale. One theory of the origin of porter was that it was a blend of ale and stout called 'alf 'n' 'alf by 18th century English porters who liked the marriage of the two styles. Later brewed as a distinct style; tastes similar to chocolate or spice.

Domestics

Anchor Porter *(California)*
Sierra Nevada Porter *(California)*
Boulder Porter *(Colorado)*
Yuengling Pottsville Porter *(Pennsylvania)*

Imports

Samuel Smith's Taddy Porter *(England)*
Young's Original London Porter *(England)*

SCOTCH ALE — similar to barley wine, scotch ales are dark and sweet with higher alcohol contents.

MacAndrews Scotch Ale *(Scotland)*
Belhaven Scottish Ale *(Scotland)*
McEwan's Scotch Ale *(Scotland)*

STOUT — very dark, heavy-bodied; can be bitter or sweet depending upon style. Dry Irish stouts like Guinness are bitter. Sweet milk stouts have maltose (candy sugar) added to create warm, delicious, liqueur taste. Roasted malts create creamy, frothy head that is almost "chewable." Stout tastes vary from coffee-like, to chocolatey, or molasses-flavored.

In Ireland, only Guinness, Murphy's and Beamish remain but stouts are also brewed in the Caribbean, West Africa and the Pacific islands where it is served slightly chilled.

Excellent cold weather or late-night beverage best enjoyed in warm surroundings with special company.

Domestics
Sierra Nevada Stout *(California)*
Boulder Stout *(Colorado)*
Hart Pyramid Sphynx Stout *(Washington)*

Imports
Guinness Irish Stout *(Ireland)*
Mackesons Triple Stout *(England)*
Sheaf Stout *(Australia)*
Beamish Stout *(Ireland)*
Murphy's Irish Stout *(Ireland)*
Samuel Smith's Oatmeal Stout *(England)*
Watney's Cream Stout *(England)*
Young's Oatmeal Stout *(England)*

The Real Beer Portfolio's specialty beers from the Young's Brewery in London, England, and the Aass Brewery in Drammen, Norway.

LAGER STYLES

Lager yeast (*saccharomyces carlsbergensis*) works at lower temperatures (45° F or below) and falls to the bottom of the brewing vessel when fermentation is complete. Storage or lagering of the beer may be at temperatures as low as 30° F for several weeks or months.

Lagers, or bottom-fermented beers, are best drunk at cooler temperatures (45-50° F) to appreciate clear, crisp taste which results from the longer, colder fermentation and storage.

AMBER — a honey-colored, German-style beer popularized by new American microbreweries. Full-bodied and well hopped, frequently with German Tettnanger, Hallertau, or Czechoslovakian Saaz hops. Rich and full tasting, generally brewed with all malted barley and no adjuncts.

Domestics

Olde Heurich (*Washington, D.C.*)
Pennsylvania Pilsner (*Pennsylvania*)
New Amsterdam (*New York*)
Samuel Adams (*Massachusetts*)
XIII Colony (*Georgia*)
Erin Brau (*Ohio*)
Christian Morlein (*Ohio*)
Reinheitsgebot Collin County (*Texas*)
Oldenberg Premium Verum (*Kentucky*)

Thousand Oaks, Berkeley, California   *Portland Lager, Portland, Oregon*

BOCK — popular seasonal beer for spring (Maibock) and fall (Oktoberfest). Brewed with darker, roasted malts to produce a sweeter and richer beer; full bodied. Bock beers frequently have a goat on the label since bock means male goat in German.

Domestic
Kessler Bock *(Montana)*
Widmer Bock *(Oregon)*

Imports
Aass Bock *(Norway)*
Ayinger Maibock *(Germany)*

DOPPELBOCK OR DOUBLE BOCK — heavier, richer malty taste due to additional malts used in brewing. Originated in Einbeck in Lower Saxony noted for brewing stronger beers and the first major commercial brewing center in Europe.

Martin Luther's favorite beer was a doppelbock. Many Bavarian doppelbock beers have suffix - ator added to their names and are quite potent.

Domestics
Samuel Adams Double Bock *(Massachusetts)*
Virginia Brewing Dobblebock *(Virginia)*

Imports
Augustiner Maximator *(Germany)*
Ayinger Celebrator *(Germany)*
Ayinger Terminator *(Germany)*
Celebrator Doppelbock *(Germany)*
E.K.U. Kulminator *(Germany)*
Paulanor Salvator *(Germany)*

DORTMUNDER — less-hopped than pilsener but darker and drier than a Munchener.

Imports
Aass Jubilee *(Norway)*
Dortmunder Kronen Export *(Germany)*

MUNCHENER — dark-colored, lightly hopped. Style developed in Munich in late 19th century. Malty taste without being too sweet.

PILSENER (PILS, PILSNER) — the most popular beer style in the world. Light body, golden-colored, slight malty taste with delicate hop aroma. Clear, crisp and generally consistent taste due to colder fermentation and long storage.

The pilsener style originated in Bohemian town of Pilsen, Czechoslovakia where soft water and local Saaz hops gave birth to this classic style. The major American, Canadian, Mexican and popular imported beers are light pilseners.

Domestics

Budweiser (*Missouri*)
Coors Banquet (*Colorado*)
Stroh's (*Michigan*)
Miller High Life (*Wisconsin*)
Lone Star (*Texas*)
Pearl (*Texas*)
Shiner (*Texas*)
Rolling Rock (*Pennsylvania*)
Iron City (*Pennsylvania*)
Saranac 1888 (*New York*)
Heileman (*Wisconsin*)
Leinenkugel (*Wisconsin*)
August Schell Pils (*Minnesota*)
Cold Spring Export (*Minnesota*)
Olympia (*Washington*)
Rainer (*Washington*)
Dixie (*Louisiana*)
Gold Cup Premium Pilsener (*Virginia*)

Imports

Molson (*Canada*)
Moosehead (*Canada*)
St. Pauli Girl (*Germany*)
Beck's (*Germany*)
Heineken (*Holland*)
Fosters (*Australia*)
Steinlager (*New Zealand*)
Kirin (*Japan*)
Sapporo (*Japan*)
Tsingtao (*China*)

Singha *(Thailand)*
Pilsner Urquell *(Czechoslovakia)*
Aass Pilsner *(Norway)*
Carta Blanca *(Mexico)*
Sol *(Mexico)*
Red Stripe *(Jamaica)*
Labatt's *(Canada)*
Carling O'Keefe *(Canada)*
Carlsberg *(Denmark)*

RAUCHBIER (Smoked) — German-style brewed with dark Bavarian malts roasted over beechwood fires. Hickory taste, long finish.

Imports
Kaiserdom Rauchbier *(Germany)*

STEAM — original California style originating from 1850s Gold Rush days when lager beer could not be stored at cold temperatures. Combines lager style bottom fermentation yeast but matured at higher temperatures in open vessels. The brand name "steam beer" has been trademarked by the San Francisco Anchor brewery.

Anchor Steam *(California)*

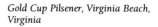

Gold Cup Pilsener, Virginia Beach, Virginia   *Vienna Lager, Milwaukee, Wisconsin*

VIENNA — reddish-colored, sweet malty style originating in Old World Vienna but now brewed in Mexico and Spanish speaking countries. Color derives from sweeter caramel malts. Vienna is sometimes called marzenbeir or marzen from a style brewed in March (Marzen) in Germany and stored in caves in the summer to drink during Oktoberfest.

Imports
Dos Equis *(Mexico)*

Domestics
Vienna All Malt Lager *(Wisconsin)*

WEISSE (Weizenbier) — wheat or "white" beer normally brewed with 50% malted wheat and 50% malted barley. Two distinct styles are the dry, sparkling Berliner Weisse and sweeter, sometimes darker-colored wheat

Specialty lagers brewed by the Munich Ayinger Brewery.

beers from Bavaria. Frequently brewed for festivals and sometimes served with twist of lemon in summer. (Dunkel or dark wheat beers use roasted malts to produce darker wheat beer.)

Domestics
Anchor Wheat (*California*)
August Schell Weiss (*Minnesota*)
Kessler Wheat (*Montana*)
Hart Pyramid Wheaten (*Washington*)
Widmer Weizenbier (*Oregon*)

Imports
Ayinger Hefe-Weissbier (*Germany*)
Ayinger Export Weiss (*Germany*)
Berliner Weisse (*Germany*)
Pinkus Original Weizen (*Germany*)
Berliner Schultheiss Weisse (*Germany*)
Hofbrauhaus Dunkelweizen (*Germany*)
Spaten Club-Weisse (*Germany*)
Paulaner Weissbier (*Germany*)
Hacker-Pschorr Weisse (*Germany*)

LAMBIC FERMENTATION

A special class of beers brewed in Belgium are the spontaneous fermentation or lambic beers. These beers are top fermented in large open vats without adding yeast. Instead, ambient yeast in the farming countryside near the brewery finds its way into the wort for "spontaneous fermentation."

Lambic beers used unmalted wheat as a major ingredient. After a primary fermentation of several days, the beer undergoes a long secondary fermentation, frequently in wooden casks which previously held wine.

Lambic beers are brewed in the Senne River Valley near Brussels in villages and on farms where brewing has been going on for centuries. Wild cherries (kriek) and raspberries (framboise) from nearby orchards are added during the secondary fermentation. The combination of the unmalted wheat, wild yeast, and fruit creates unique beers; they have been compared to a fruity wine but with a dry, champagne-like effervescence.

Lambic beers can be served as aperitifs or to accompany foods and desserts where distinction is the objective. Their lactic character makes them highly recommended for special occasions.

> **Liefman's** *(Belgium)*
> **Lindemans** *(Belgium)*
> **Mort Subite** *(Belgium)*
> **Timmermans** *(Belgium)*

Specialty beers imported by Phoenix Imports of Baltimore, Maryland. Hurlimann's Samichlaus (Santa Claus) from Switzerland; Eldridge Pope's Royal Oak and Thomas Hardy Ale from Dorchester, England; Liefman's Kriek (cherry), Framboise (raspberry) and Goudenband (brown ale) from Belgium; Corsendonk's Brown Ale (Belgium).

SEASONAL AND CHRISTMAS BEERS

A wonderful tradition is being revived by progressive breweries — the brewing of seasonal and Christmas specialty beers. Seasonal beers include springtime bock beers and festival beers for fall and Octoberfest celebrations. Once a normal part of a European brewery's operations, the crafting of seasonal and Christmas beers are enjoying such popularity in America that even mainstream breweries like Coors are getting into the holiday spirit.

Coors of Golden, Colorado, became the first major American brewery to market a Christmas beer, "Winterfest," nationwide in 1987.

Two of California's premier craft breweries, Anchor and Sierra Nevada, vintage date their Christmas beer. Both are superb products and represent the highest state of brewing as an art.

Most Christmas beers are ales brewed with darker, sweeter malts. Cinnamon, allspice, nutmeg and other spices are added to create festive tastes. If a few bottles can be saved into the New Year, Christmas beers are excellent for cooking if the cook will forego cellaring them to serve for special guests. The Swiss brewer Hurlimann's Samichlaus (Santa Claus) has earned a place in the Guinness Book of Records as the most potent beer (11% alcohol by weight). Samichlaus is brewed only on December 6, St. Nicholas Day, with special yeast able to survive the high alcohol content. Secondary fermentation may take as long as 10 months before bottling.

Many North American microbreweries are brewing Christmas beers and changing the recipes every year. Their efforts have been very popular festive beers even though the supply is limited.

Domestics

Anchor Christmas Ale *(California)*
Sierra Nevada Celebration Ale *(California)*
Coors Winterfest *(Colorado)*
Independent Winterhook *(Washington)*

Imports

Nochebuena *(Mexico)*
Hurlimann's Samichlaus *(Switzerland)*
Aass Winter *(Norway)*
Young's Winter Warmer *(England)*

Young's Winter Ale 1988
Young's Brewery
London, England

CHAPTER FOUR

THE BREWPUB BONANZA

C hances are, one of these days you'll walk into a restaurant and notice something different. Maybe it will be the steamy aroma of grain cooking, or the shiny copper and stainless steel kettles gleaming in the window. When you notice someone wearing rubber boots stirring the kettles with a paddle, the thought may cross your mind — is this a restaurant or a brewery?

Actually, it's a "brewpub" — a brewery in a restaurant. Brewpubs are part of the nationwide microbrewing movement that many observers say is quietly revolutionizing the entire brewing industry. According to experts, brewpubs also may be leading another revolution — in the restaurant industry.

Along with the smell of fresh bread baking, the aroma of beer brewing is one of life's culinary pleasures. The warm, moist aroma of steaming hops and barley is enough to arouse a non-beer drinker's thirst. Fresh, creamy beer with a rocky head and perfumy hop aroma is the product of a craftsman. It's the result of approaching brewing as an art — with passion and sensitivity endeavoring to produce a memorable, pleasurable experience.

Buffalo Bill's the second brewpub in California, opened in 1983.

The Weeping Radish Brewpub on North Carolina's Outer Banks.

A HUMBLE BEGINNING

If major lifestyle trends were required to have humble origins, brewpubs certainly would qualify. In the summer of 1982, veteran brewer Bert Grant opened a little pub brewery, the Yakima Brewing and Malting Company, in a converted opera house a few miles from the Washington fields where most of America's hops are grown. Grant brewed English and Scottish ales and sold them like they do in Great Britain — in a pub complete with dart board, "pub food," and crests of Scottish clans adorning the walls.

While the brewing barons in St. Louis, Pittsburgh, and Milwaukee scratched their heads, legions of homebrewers, beer enthusiasts and '60s type free spirits flocked to Yakima. They listened to Grant like he was the new Mahareeshi talk about making small batches of specialty beers and selling them in brewpub restaurants. Grant had seen the future and it was full of hops and barley. A brewing concept was being reborn in America: small-scale, craft brewing in a restaurant. The English have had the brewpubs for centuries; so have the Germans.

Within a year, Grant's disciples opened brewpubs in Northern California, British Columbia and Oregon, with customers standing in line to taste the fresh beer. The media fell in love with brewpubs and reports about them appeared in almost every West Coast newspaper, magazine, and on TV and radio. The brewpub stories had what every editor and producer lusts after — local charm, a fun product, entrepreneurism, and an eccentric pioneer. It was the journalistic equivalent to finding a new Thomas Edison in a garage with his wild hair and funny little bulb.

BEER LIKE GRANDPA
AND GRANDMA USED TO DRINK

And by the way, the beer was pretty good. Not the bland, yellow fizz piled in stacks at supermarket and drug store chains alongside the tires and laundry detergent. This was real beer with fruity hops, full body, a frothy head and an aroma and taste like nothing brewed in America since Prohibition.

The brewpub types even gave their beer colorful names like Maid Marion Ale, Ruby Tuesday, Pelican Pale, Tasmanian Devil, City Lights, Lucky Stars, Calistoga Lager, Redhook ESB, Golden Gate Lager, Mt. Tolmie Dark, Iron Horse Ale, Hogshead Lager, Emperor North, Blue Heron Ale, High Roller Wheat, Old Knucklehead Barleywine, and Punkin Ale. You can't keep a good idea like this quiet for long —

California's first brewpub, the Mendocino Brewing, opened in Hopland in 1983.

Napa Valley's first brewpub at the Calistoga Inn.

particularly when that good idea is about beer, which 80 million Americans drink almost every day. After "yuppies" got turned on to gourmet yogurt, ice cream, and cookies, how could you lose with gourmet beer? Within five years enterprising restaurateurs opened brewpubs in New York, North Carolina, Wisconsin, Pennsylvania and Virginia.

Twelve years after the first microbrewery appeared in a Sonoma, California, warehouse, the movement had grown to 250 microbreweries and brewpubs in North America. The Colorado-based Association of Brewers publication, "New Brewer," predicts their numbers may total 1000 by the mid 1990s.

The brewpub movement is booming on the West Coast. In just seven years after the first brewpub opened in Yakima, Washington in 1982, more than forty brewpubs had opened from San Diego to Seattle with thirteen in the San Francisco Bay area alone.

But "pubbrewers" optimism does not come from past growth figures — their real enthusiasm is in future projections. "There will be 2,000 brewpubs in California alone by the year 2000," says Californian Bill Owens, who owns three brewpubs (Buffalo Bill's in Hayward, Brewery on the Green in Fremont, and The Bison in Berkeley). "It won't be long until you'll be able to drive the Pacific Coast Highway all the way from San Diego to Eureka and never be more than 10 minutes away from a brewpub," predicts Owens who could be the first to launch a national brewpub franchise.

Cornelius Pass Roadhouse and The Lighthouse, two of Oregon's first brewpubs.

PENNIES TO BREW . . . DOLLARS TO SELL . . .

Brewpubs are a separate profit center for a restaurant. The costs of production (hops, barley, equipment, salaries) are modest (pennies per glass) and the return ($1.50/3.00 for a 12 oz. draft) is high. With ingenuity, profits can be squeezed from a brewpub in a way they can't from a restaurant. The key is to brew a distinctive, flavorful beer and not the gassy, industrial-brewed beer that has been called "liquid air" and less polite names in circles where good beer has become a cult.

With such delightful names as the Tap and Growler (Chicago), Weeping Radish (Manteo, North Carolina), Oldenberg Brewery (Ft. Mitchell, Kentucky), and Sherlock's Home (Minnetonka, Minnesota), brewpubs have returned the charm and romance to brewing in America that had all but disappeared. They've also rekindled a thirst for specialty beers — amber lagers, ales, porters, stouts, bock, wheat and seasonal holiday beers for Oktoberfest and Christmas.

Goose Island Brewery and Siebens River North, two of Chicago's first brewpubs, opened in 1988.

A BREWPUB FRANCHISING BOOM COMING

"Brewpub restaurants brewing their own beer will be the hottest franchising trend in the 1990s," franchising consultant Gary Kisel told an audience of microbrewers at their annual convention in Chicago in 1988. "Within ten years there will be 100 regional chains with ten to twelve brewpubs apiece," Kisel forecast. "There also will be two or three national chains with at least sixty brewpubs apiece."

Kisel was not the only restaurant consultant making such lavish predictions at that convention. "Everybody in the restaurant and hotel trade now is taking a look at brewpubs and wanting to get into the business," echoed Phil Kralovec of the Chicago-based National Restaurant Association. "The Hyatt Hotels have a brewpub and will be going nationwide soon. They're not the only big chain that's going to get involved."

Laurel Hanson, former general manager of Chicago's first brewpub, Siebens River North, was just as optimistic. "Once a restaurant discovers the costs of making beer — 24% — they'll want to put in a little brewpub to increase their profits. Food costs are much higher than that."

Chicago is the first major city outside the West Coast to become a center for brewing specialty beers. Four brewpubs have started up in Chicago and the legendary downtown Berghoff restaurant purchased Wisconsin's Huber brewery in 1988 to make its beer.

But Chicago isn't the only city scrambling in the barley bonanza. New brewpubs have opened or soon will in Charlotte, Des Moines, Omaha, San Jose, Burlington, Buffalo, Missoula, Atlanta, Seattle, Denver, Minneapolis, Phoenix, and Winter Park.

Can Peoria be far behind?

COMING TO YOUR NEIGHBORHOOD SOON . . .

A nationwide brewpub bonanza is coming. Bert Grant, Bill Owens and their microbrewing colleagues are hustling to cash in before the restaurant chains put a brewpub in every shopping mall and prime downtown location around the country. They know the next wave will bring a flood of accountants, franchisers, hotel chains, advertising moguls and venture capitalists. Beer won't be just "beer" anymore — it'll be the biggest thing to happen to the brewing industry since the Repeal of Prohibition.

Oldenberg Premium Verum
Oldenberg Brewery
Fort Mitchell, Kentucky

NORTH AMERICAN BREWPUBS
UNITED STATES

ARIZONA

Bandersnatch Brewpub
125 E. 5th Avenue
Tempe   602-966-4438

CALIFORNIA

Anderson Valley
14081 Highway 128
Boonville   707-895-2337

Biers Brasserie
33 E. San Fernando Street
San Jose   408-297-3766

Bison Brewing
2598 Telegraph Avenue
Berkeley   415-841-7734

Brewpub on the Green
3350 Stevenson Blvd
Fremont   415-651-5510

Buffalo Bill's Brewpub
1082 B Street
Hayward   415-886-9823

Butterfield Brewery
777 East Olive
Fresno   209-264-5521

City of Angels Brewery
1445 4th Street
Santa Monica   213-451-0096

Crown City Brewery
300 S. Raymond
Pasadena   818-577-5548

Dead Cat Alley Brewery
667 Dead Cat Alley
Woodland

Devil Mountain Brewery
850 South Broadway
Walnut Creek   415-935-2337

Emery Pub & Brewery
5800 Shell Mound
Emeryville   415-653-0444

Golden Gate
1 Bolivar Drive
Berkeley   415-644-9885

Gordon-Biersch
640 Emerson Street
Palo Alto   415-323-7723

Gorky's Cafe and Brewery
536 E. 8th Street
Los Angeles   213-459-4805

Grapevine Brewery
658 Legec Road
Lebec   805-248-6890

Hogshead Brewpub
114 J Street
Sacramento   916-443-2739

Humboldt Brewery
856 10th Street
Arcata   707-826-2739

Kelmer's Brewhouse
458 B Street
Santa Rosa   707-544-4677

Mammoth Lakes Brewing
170 Mountain Blvd
Mammoth Lakes   619-934-8134

Marin Brewing
1809 Larkspur Landing Circle
Larkspur   415-461-4677

Monterey Brewing
700 Cannery Row
Monterey   408-375-3634

Napa Valley Brewing/Calistoga Inn
1250 Lincoln Avenue
Calistoga   707-942-4101

North Coast Brewing
444 N. Main
Ft. Bragg   707-964-2739

Karl Strauss' Old Columbia
    Brewery & Grill
2810 Mission Blvd
San Diego   619-488-4241

Pacific Coast Brewing
906 Washington
Oakland   415-836-2739

Rubicon Brewing
2004 Capitol Avenue
Sacramento   916-488-7032

San Andreas Brewing
737 San Benito
Hollister   408-637-7074

San Francisco Brewing
155 Columbus Avenue
San Francisco   415-434-3344

Santa Cruz Brewing/Front Street Pub
516 Front Street
Santa Cruz   408-429-8838

Seabright Brewing
519 Seabright Ave
Santa Cruz   408-426-2739

Seacliff Cafe & Vest Pocket Brewery
1801 Clement
San Francisco   415-386-6266

SLO Brewing
1119 Garden Street
San Luis Obispo   805-543-1843

Tied House Cafe and Brewery
954 Villa
Mountain View   415-965-2739

Triple Rock Brewing
1920 Shattuck
Berkeley   415-843-2739

Truckee Brewing
Truckee   916-587-7411

Willett's Brewery
902 Main
Napa   707-258-2337

Winchester Brewing
820 S. Winchester
San Jose   408-243-7561

COLORADO

Carver Brewing
1022 Main
Durango   719-259-2545

Wynkoop Brewing
1634 18th Street
Denver   303-297-2700

FLORIDA

McGuire's Irish Pub
600 E. Gregory Street
Pensacola   904-433-6789

Winter Park Brewing
330 West Fairbanks
Winter Park   407-644-0022

Zum Alten Fritz/Miami Brewpub
1828-1840 NE 4th Avenue
Miami   305-358-5731

GEORGIA

Highland Brewery
816 North Highland
Atlanta   404-876-7115

IDAHO

Coeur D'Alene Brewing
204 North 2nd Street
Coeur D'Alene   208-664-2739

ILLINOIS

Goose Island
1800 N. Clybourn
Chicago   312-915-0071

Sieben Brewing/River North
436 W. Ontario
Chicago   312-787-7313

Tap & Growler
901 West Jackson
Chicago   312-829-1599

Weinkeller Brewery
6417 W. Roosevelt Boulevard
Berwyn   312-749-2276

KANSAS

Free State Brewing
636 Massachusetts
Lawrence   913-843-4555

KENTUCKY

Oldenberg Brewery
I 75 at Buttermilk Pike
Ft. Michell   606-341-2800

MAINE

Gritty McDuff's
396 Fore Street
Portland   207-772-2739

MARYLAND

Sisson's
36 E. Cross Street
Baltimore   301-539-2093

MASSACHUSETTS

Cambridge Brewing
1 Kendall Square
Cambridge   617-494-1994

Commonwealth Brewing
85 Merrimac Street
Boston   617-523-8383

Northampton Brewery
11 Brewster Ct.
Northampton   413-584-9903

MINNESOTA

Sherlock's Home
11000 Red Circle Drive
Minnetonka   612-931-0203

Taps Waterfront Brewpub
25 Main Street, SE
Minneapolis   612-623-0923

MONTANA

Bayern Brewing
Northern Pacific Depot
Missoula   406-721-2739

NEVADA

Union Brewery
28 North C Street
Virginia City   702-847-0328

NEW MEXICO

Preston Brewery
P.O. Box 154
Embudo   505-852-4707

NEW YORK

Buffalo Brewpub
6861 Main Street
Williamsville   716-632-0552

Manhattan Brewing
40-42 Thompson Street
New York   212-219-9250

Rochester Brewpub
800 Jefferson
Henrietta   716-272-1550

NORTH CAROLINA

Dilworth Brewing
1301 East Boulevard
Charlotte   704-377-2739

Weeping Radish
P.O. Box 1471
Manteo   919-473-1991

Weeping Radish #2
115 N. Duke Street
Durham   919-682-2337

OHIO

Great Lakes Brewing
2516 Market Street
Cleveland   216-771-4404

Growler's Brewpub
2221 Wagoner-Ford Road
Dayton   513-275-0035

OREGON

Bay Front Brewery
248 Bay Boulevard
Newport   503-265-3188

Cornelius Pass Roadhouse
Rt. 5
Hillsboro   503-640-6174

Deschutes Public House
1044 Bond Street, NW
Bend   503-382-9242

Fulton Pub
618 SW Nebraska
Portland   503-246-9530

High Street Pub
1243 High Street
Eugene   503-345-4905

Highland
4225 SE 182nd Ave.
Gresham   503-665-3015

Hillsdale Public House
1505 SW Sunset Boulevard
Portland   503-246-3938

Lighthouse Brew-Pub
4157 N. Highway 101
Lincoln City   503-994-7238

Rogue River Brewing
31-B Water Street
Ashland   503-488-5061

PENNSYLVANIA

Stoudt Brewery
P.O. Box 809
Adamstown   215-484-4387

VERMONT

Vermont Pub & Brewery
144 College Street
Burlington   802-865-0500

VIRGINIA

Blue Ridge Brewing
709 West Main
Charlottesville   804-977-0017

WASHINGTON

Big Time Brewing
4133 University Way, SE
Seattle   206-545-4509

Noggins Westlake Brewpub
400 Pine Street
Seattle   206-682-2739

Noggins Brewpub at Brooklyn Square
4142 Brooklyn Avenue, NE
Seattle   206-682-2739

WISCONSIN

Brewmaster's Pub
4017 80th Street
Kenosha   414-694-9050

Oliver's Station
341 North Third Ave
Sturgeon Bay   414-746-0900

Water Street
1101 North Water Street
Milwaukee   414-272-1195

CANADA

ALBERTA

Boccalino Pasta Bistro
10525 Jasper Avenue
Edmonton   403-462-7313

BRITISH COLUMBIA

Leeward Neighbourhood Pub
649 Anderton Road
Comox   604-339-5400

Prairie Inn Cottage Brewery
7806 E. Saanich Road
Saanichton   604-652-1575

Spinnakers
308 Catherine Street
Victoria   604-384-6613

NOVA SCOTIA

Granite Brewery
P.O. Box 114
Halifax   902-422-4954

ONTARIO

Amsterdam Brasserie & Brewpub
133 John Street
Toronto   416-595-8201

Atlas Hotel
35 Southworth St. N
Welland   416-732-5054

Blue Anchor
47 West St. SE
Orillia   705-327-7000

Charley's Tavern
4715 Tecumseh Road East
Windsor   519-945-5512

Heidelberg Brewery
2 King Street
Heidelberg   519-699-4413

Houston/Tracks
60 Queen Street East
Brampton   416-453-3800

Jolly Friar Brasserie and Brewpub
320 Bay Street
Sault Saint Marie   705-945-8888

Kingston Brewing
34 Clarence Street
Kingston   613-542-4978

The Lion Brewery & Museum
Huether Hotel, 59 King Street N.
Waterloo   519-886-3350

Luxembourg Brewpub
4230 Sherwoodtowne Boulevard
Mississauga   416-897-2739

Master's Brasserie & Brewpub
330 Queen Street
Ottawa   613-594-3688

Mr. Grumpp's Restaurant
9737 Yonge Street
Richmond Hill   416-883-4840

Port Arthur Brasserie & Brewpub
901 Red River Road
Thunder Bay   807-767-4415

Queen's Inn/Taylor & Bate, Ltd.
161 Ontario Street
Stratford   519-271-1400

Rotterdam Brewing
600 King Street
Toronto   416-868-6882

Tapsters Brewhouse
100 Brittania Road East
Mississauga   416-890-8909

Winchester Arms
255 Dundas Street West
Mississauga   416-897-1481

QUEBEC

Le Bar Cervoise
4457 Blvd. St. Laurent
Montreal   514-843-6586

Le Cheval Blanc
809 Ontario Street
Montreal   512-522-0211

Crocodile Club
5414 Gatineau
Montreal   514-733-2125

Mon Village Brewery
2760 Cote Street, Charles Road
Hudson   514-458-5331

CHAPTER FIVE

BEER TASTING DINNERS

T he revolution in specialty beers has reached the kitchen.
 In restaurants, hotels and country clubs where wine tastings and wine dinners were regularly scheduled, chefs are being called upon to show their creativity in cooking with specialty beers. Restaurants in Europe — particularly in Belgium — have been cooking with beer for decades and the practice finally is being adopted by progressive restaurants in America.

Fine restaurants in New York, Washington, Chicago, Seattle and San Francisco are enthusiastically promoting beer dinners and preparing elaborate menus: monkfish with carmelized onions served with Samuel Adams Boston Lager; shrimp and scallop stew cooked with Paulaner Pilsener; carbonnade of beef made with Samuel Smith's Imperial Stout; marinated duck with Samuel Smith's Pale Ale; fruit tart with Liefmans' Framboise.

Whether this is the beginning of a new trend or a revival of an old tradition, the benefits of featuring specialty beers at special events in restaurants is likely to find an appreciative following among customers. A hamburger with a beer takes little imagination to behold; a spicy ale served with jambalaya or barbecued ribs will awaken many a dulled appetite.

A SERIES OF DINNERS FEATURING SPECIALTY BEERS

While researching this book, I was invited by several restaurants on the East Coast to arrange dinners and tastings featuring specialty beers. The events ranged from introductory "blind" tastings with appetizers to elaborate four-course dinners featuring Christmas beers.

The initial invitation came from a neighborhood restaurant in Alexandria, Virginia, the Calvert Grille, owned by Lynn and Don Abram, the daughter and son-in-law of a friend, Mike Abraham, who runs the Vienna Inn, in Vienna, Virginia. Lynn, Don, and I came up with three dinners in the summer and fall featuring specialty beers from North America, Europe and Asia. Don prepared menus for the dinners which varied with the beer selection we chose.

This initial series was followed by another series of three dinners at the Waters Edge restaurant in Cape May, a popular summer tourist resort at the southern tip of New Jersey. Neil Elshon, the chef and owner, prepared an elaborate menu for each dinner and his wife, Karen, shared host duties while I moderated the dinner.

A spring beer dinner, Tony & Joe's Washington, D.C.

Since most patrons had not been to a beer dinner and probably knew little about specialty beers, I prepared a 50-point rating sheet (see end of chapter) for them to evaluate each beer's aroma, body, color and taste. After I made some preliminary remarks about brewing and rating beers, the patrons started with welcoming beers and appetizers and proceeded to the entree and dessert — all accompanied with three or four beers per course. I related anecdotes about microbreweries and specialty beers from my travels and research while the patrons tasted, judged, and commented on the food and beer.

The response was overwhelming! Many said they had been to wine tastings and dinners, but had never been to an event featuring specialty beers and food. They loved having beer styles matched to specific foods and talked about planning a similar event at home with friends (see chapter 6).

I kept the atmosphere at the dinners informal which allowed the patrons the opportunity to share their experiences and knowledge of beer. Everyone seems to have a favorite beer story and a beer dinner is a suitable occasion to share a story or two.

Although beer is the most popular alcohol beverage in America, few Americans are knowledgeable about beer. Even some who considered themselves experts were startled when they found out how they rated the beers in a blind tasting. Several who professed that they drank only a certain standard domestic or imported beer were surprised when they rated them the lowest! Some — particularly women — who said they didn't even care for beer, were amazed at the rich variety and taste in specialty ales and lagers and became converts after just one tasting.

PLANNING A MENU FOR A BEER DINNER

The dinners at the Calvert Grille and Waters Edge led to other invitations from restaurants to do similar events. I developed four distinct dinner themes to show the diversity in specialty beers and menus: a standard international; a North American; a microbrewery; and a Christmas or festival event.

The introductory dinner was a blind tasting of a dozen beers served with appetizer-style foods. The menu and beer selection varied greatly after this initial tasting and many chefs came up with their own recipes using beer.

Since it was the first time many restaurants had planned a beer dinner, I recommended the initial menu be easy to prepare and serve:

APPETIZER
Smoked turkey, chicken, or seafood

BEERS SERVED
American, Canadian, Mexican, German lagers

ENTREES
Choice of spicy sausage, chili, jambalaya,
beef stew, barbecued ribs

BEERS SERVED
American, English, Australian ales

DESSERT
Pastry, cheese and fruit platter

BEERS SERVED
Stouts, lambic, festival beers

Food married with beer in a restaurant setting is a novel way to introduce patrons to specialty beers and fine cuisine. Once weaned from popular domestic and imported brands, customers will find specialty beers an exciting addition to cuisine.

ARE WOMEN THE BEST JUDGES OF BEER?

One of the delights at the beer dinners was the number of women who attended and their enthusiastic participation. Womens' palates seem to be more sensitive to the subtle tastes and aromas in specialty beers.

Women frequently were more articulate than the men they accompanied in discussing beer. Men, on the other hand, were both delighted by the women's appreciation for the beers, but chagrined that they were more articulate in describing them. If the dinners were any indication of the future, men may have precious little time left to consider themselves beer authorities. Women are great beer lovers!

BEER DINNER MENUS

$$\boxed{1}$$

MICROBREWERY TASTING
CALVERT GRILLE
ALEXANDRIA, VA

APPETIZER
Smoked chicken

BEERS
New Amsterdam, Olde Heurich, Acme

ENTREES
Chili, Barbecued Ribs

BEERS
Anchor Steam, Sierra Nevada Pale Ale, Boulder Pale Ale

DESSERT
Cheese & Fruit Platter

BEERS
August Schell Wheat, Dock Street, Bigfoot Barley Wine

CHEF: Don Abram

2

INTERNATIONAL TASTING
OLD EBBIT GRILLE
WASHINGTON, D.C.

APPETIZER
Indonesian Chicken Satay
char grilled and served with Spicy Peanut Sauce

BEERS
Budweiser, Olde Heurich, Heineken

ENTREE
Spicy Sausage baked in Brown Ale

BEERS
Fullers ESB, Anchor Liberty Ale, Bios Copper Ale

DESSERT
Fruit & Cheese Platter: Strawberries, Melons, Kiwi, Grapes
White Cheddar, English Stilton, Aged Provolone

BEERS
Sierra Nevada Porter, Lindeman Framboise
Cooper Stout, Mackeson Stout

CHEF: Tom Meyer

3

MID-WINTER BEER DINNER
WATER'S EDGE
CAPE MAY, NJ

APERITIF BEER
Fischer's La Belle Strasbourgeoise

APPETIZER
Shrimp and Avocado Enchilada
with Spicy Tomato-Cilantro Salsa

BEERS
Dos Equis

SALAD
Seasonal Green Salad
Sun-dried Tomato Vinaigrette

BEERS
Harp Lager

ENTREES
Roast Chicken with Herbed Crust and Ale Supreme Sauce
Garlic and Porter Mashed Potatoes
Braised Cabbages with Rice Wine Vinegar

BEERS
Dock Street Amber Beer, Boulder Stout

DESSERT
Raspberry Cream Puffs with Chocolate Glaze

BEERS
Lindeman's Framboise

CHEF: Neil Elshon

4

BRITISH BEER TASTING
SILO RESTAURANT
STERLING, VA

APPETIZER
Smoked Chicken & Water Biscuits

BEERS
Young's Special London Ale, John Courage

ENTREE
Top Round of Beef, Green Beans, Mushrooms

BEERS
Olde Heurich Amber Lager, Newcastle Brown Ale

DESSERT
Fruit and Cheese Platter with Tea Biscuits

BEERS
McEwan Scotch Ale, Belhaven, Royal Oak

Hosting a British beer dinner, the Silo Restaurant, Sterling, Virginia.

$$\boxed{5}$$

INTERNATIONAL TASTING WITH SEAFOOD
TONY & JOE'S
WASHINGTON, D.C.

APPETIZERS
Broiled Oysters stuffed with Spinach & Crabmeat
in a Pernod Cream Sauce
Grilled Scallops wrapped in Bacon with Lemon Caper Butter
Steamed Mussels with Spicy Ale Sauce in Garlic Pepper Butter

BEERS
Coors, Heineken, Olde Heurich, Anchor Steam

ENTREES
Zucchini stuffed with Cajun Crabmeat & Crawfish
Sauteed Snapper in Spicy Flour Butter topped with
Mushroom & Oyster Cream Sauce

BEERS
Young's Special London Ale, Dock Street, Coopers Real Ale, Duvel

DESSERT
Cheese & Fruit Platter

BEERS
Mackeson Stout, Cooper's Stout, Lindeman's Framboise,
Newcastle Brown Ale

CHEF: Damian Salvatore

SUGGESTIONS FOR RESTAURANTS PLANNING BEER TASTING DINNER

1. Choose eight to twelve beers from the range of styles: lagers, ales, porters and stout to offer customers diversity. Serve beers from light in body, color and texture to heavier, darker and more complex. (Example: Proceed from pale pilsener, to amber lagers, to ales, porters, lambic, and stout.)

2. Work with a distributor to choose beers customers may not be familiar with, i.e., beers not heavily advertised and promoted.

3. If possible, do the tasting "blind" so you are educating customers and not just serving them beers they know.

4. Serve beers in clean glasses; each beer gets a clean glass.

5. When washing glasses, don't use detergent for last wash. Detergent leaves a film which can influence subtle tastes and aromas.

6. Take beer out of refrigerator about fifteen minutes before tasting so they can be cool but not cold. Don't serve beers ice cold or in frosted glasses.

7. Pour about 2 oz. per glass and serve quickly.

8. Remove empty glasses from table but let glasses with beer remain. Patrons like to compare color of beers during tasting.

9. If possible, have a rating sheet for patrons to evaluate beers and write comments. The sheet also makes for a handy promotion to advertise special events and future beer tastings or dinners.

10. Have someone knowledgeable about specialty beers serve as moderator or host. Patrons like to have someone explain the event and answer questions about beers and foods.

SERVING FOOD

1. For your first tasting choose foods that don't place a burden on your kitchen or waitstaff. Three platters of appetizer, entree and dessert are sufficient.

2. Serve platters one per table with small plates at each setting for patrons to serve themselves.

3. Have plenty of bread and ice water at each table. Beer tasting is a thirsty calling and palates need cleansing during the evening.

4. Schedule an event early in the evening (6:00-7:00 PM) since the tasting will take a couple hours if done properly. Customers will have plenty of food, bread, beer and water during a tasting and shouldn't be hungry when it's over.

5. Caution customers not to eat all the food as soon as it is placed on the table. Each platter should last for 2-4 beers depending upon how many you serve.

Chinook Alaskan Amber Beer
Chinook Alaskan Brewery
Juneau, Alaska

Most Popular Beer
in America 1988
Great American Beer Festival

BEER-TASTING SCORE SHEET

WHAT TO LOOK FOR IN A BEER
(1 point is the lowest score)

1. Color: (1-5 points)

2. Head Retention: (1-5)

3. Hop Aroma, Bouquet: (1-10)

4. Initial Taste: (1-10)

5. Mouth Feel: (1-10)

6. Lasting Taste: (1-10)

DESIRABLE FEATURES

- golden, amber, ruby, chocolately
- height, durability, bubbles, "legs"
- flowery, fruity, nutty, hoppy
- bitter, malty, smoky, fruity
- full bodied, round
- complex, long finish

UNDESIRABLE FEATURES

- cloudy, washed-out, hazy
- flat, weak,
- nonexistent
- gassy, bland, weak
- watery, thin
- short finish

Highest possible score is 50 points
Outstanding — 45 to 50 points
Highly Recommended — 40 to 44 points
Average — 30 to 39 points
Below Average — 29 points or less

Beer No.	Name	Rating Categories						Total Score
		1	2	3	4	5	6	

Copyright © Jack Erickson

PHOTO BY MING LEONG

Rating beers at a "blind" tasting.

CHAPTER SIX

PLANNING A BEER DINNER AT HOME

N ow that you've learned a little bit about beer and how it is featured in restaurants with food, why not plan a beer dinner at home?
You'll be trying some of the recipes in the next section of the book, so
consider planning a menu and invite friends for a "special" beer dinner.

But before you schedule a beer dinner, you might want to have a beer
tasting to find out about these beers and how they go with foods. And
as long as you're going to be tasting some exciting beers, why not invite
a couple friends and make it a little party?

An informal beer tasting can be as much fun as a beer dinner itself
and help everyone involved learn about beer styles and foods. All it takes
is a little preparation, a shopping trip to a liquor store, a few friends,
a note pad — and a sense of adventure. After the tasting you'll know
which foods you want to serve, the beers to go with them, and how to
introduce them to your guests.

AN INFORMAL BEER TASTING

A beer tasting begins with a shopping trip. If you live in or near a
major city, you should be able to find specialty beers at a gourmet food
store, supermarket or liquor store. A store's beverage manager might offer
suggestions if finding specialty beers proves difficult. You might want to
show him or her this book and mention that you'd like to see a wider
selection of specialty beers.

The beers you select should represent several styles: pale pilsener, amber lagers, bock, pale or brown ales, porter, sweet and dry stout, wheat, lambic, and seasonal beers such as Oktoberfest or Christmas beers. One from each style will give you about ten to taste — enough for your first tasting. You'll need a single bottle of each beer since you'll be serving only two or three ounces per person.

There are generally four factors to consider when choosing beers for a tasting or a dinner — aroma, body, taste and color. Specialty beers generally are more full-bodied, complex, and tastier than "industrial-brewed" beers. You'll notice the difference right away if this is your first venture into tasting specialty beers. Lagers are crisp and clean tasting; ales tend to be "hoppy" and spicy; porters dark and flavorful; stouts heavier and assertive; bock and seasonal beers dark and complex; lambic sweet and "winey."

Consider the color of the beers in making your choice. Before sensing even the first hint of a hop aroma, your eyes will "drink" the beer's color. A rich, deep, or clear color is certainly going to be more pleasing than a washed out or faded color. What table would not be enhanced by the presence of a golden-colored Belgian Maes Pils, a copper-colored Young's Special London Ale, a mellow-brown Celebrator double bock, or a black-as-coal Australian Sheaf Stout? You'll appreciate the range of colors the first time your table is graced by a row of glasses filled with these beautiful beers.

GETTING READY

A successful tasting — even an informal one — requires a little preparation. You'll need extra glasses so that each beer can be tasted in a clean glass. Six to eight-ounce wine glasses are preferable since they allow the eye to examine the color and the nose to smell the bouquet. Beer mugs, steins or opaque glasses are inappropriate for a proper tasting.

Wash and rinse your tasting glasses in hot water without detergent. Commercial soaps leave a film residue that can interfere with tasting the subtleties of these beers.

Take the beers out of the refrigerator about ten minutes before you're ready to begin. Beers served ice cold or chilled shock the taste buds and stunt your ability to taste them properly. Beer should be a cool, tantalizing presence on the palate — not a shock.

Beer tasting also stimulates the appetite. As a host or hostess, you'll want to serve basic foods to your fellow tasters. A selection of meats — smoked turkey, chicken, fish, roast beef, pork, ham — and a platter of cheese, fruits, and a dessert will help you and your friends make some basic match-ups with the beers. Most of these foods can be picked up or prepared without much difficulty.

Have bread or unsalted crackers and a pitcher of cold water on the table for your guests. The bread or crackers will cleanse the palate between beers; the water slackens the thirst and refreshes the mouth. Beer tasting is "thirsty" work.

START WITH A PILSENER, LAGER, PALE ALE . . .

Open beers one at a time, starting with the pale pilseners and amber lagers. Since you'll want to be as "sharp" on the last beer as you are on the first, serve only a couple ounces per beer. Your friends only need to taste the beer to decide if they like the hoppiness, maltiness, aroma, taste, and mouth feel.

Proceed a beer at a time through the ales, porters, stouts, and seasonal beers, keeping a note pad to write your comments and suggestions. Your memory may get a little fuzzy along about the eighth or ninth beer and you'll want notes when you go shopping for the beers for your dinner.

With each beer try one or two foods. For example, start with a pale pilsener, amber lager or pale ale and taste the smoked turkey, chicken, or fish. Write down your impressions and go on to another beer and try the same foods. The process isn't difficult, just remember to make notes and don't fill up on food too early; you'll want to save your palate and appetite for the dessert beers, fruits, and cheeses at the end.

The darker beers should be tasted with darker or spicier meats. Save the seasonal and lambic beers for the cheese, fruit, and dessert platter.

After two hours you should have a table full of empty glasses, bottles, crumbs and stained notes from the tasting. You and your friends can congratulate each other; you're "experts" in specialty beers and ready for the main event.

PLANNING A BEER DINNER

After an informal tasting you'll be ready to plan a menu and beers to serve with your beer dinner — from appetizers and salads through entrees and desserts.

First of all, a reassuring note — there are no hard and formal rules about matching beer with food like there are with wine. The only rule to follow is to choose what you prefer and what you think your guests will like. But before you put those beers on your dinner table, you'll want to be sure they've met your standards in taste and compatibility — that's what the tasting will have accomplished.

When selecting beers for your dinner you might want to consider the following basic foods and beer styles:

> **Seafood** — pale pilsener, amber lager or spicy ale
>
> **Shellfish** — porter, stout
>
> **Poultry** — amber lager, ale
>
> **Pork, veal, beef** — amber lager, brown ale
>
> **Game meat** — Scottish ale, porter, dry stout
>
> **Roasts and stews** — amber lager, porter, stout
>
> **Cheese dishes and desserts** — pale ale, porter, sweet stout, lambics

Beer To Cut, Complement, Or Contrast Food

A friend and beer connoisseur, Dane Wells, has developed a 3 "C" system of matching beers with food. Dane, along with his wife Joan, is proprietor of the Queen Victoria Inn in Cape May, New Jersey, and a certified beer judge. When cooking or serving beer with food, Dane uses the three "C" options, i.e., selecting beers to cut, complement, and contrast the food.

For example, Dane will "cut" the flavor of a rich creamy sauce with a beer that is tart or slightly bitter (a Berlinerweisse or pilsener with lobster cream sauce). Dane's complementary beer would be an assertive beer with spicy food (smoked fowl or fish with a rauchbier). Dane's contrast beer is a spicy or robust style with bland food, (oyster with stout).

Finding The Right Marriage In Beer And Food

A general guideline to follow is to start your beer dinner with lighter colored beers and proceed to darker beers. Before dinner, a wonderful aperitif would be a lambic cherry or raspberry beer or a wheat beer with a lemon in summer.

A salad or appetizer course would feature a pilsener, amber lager, or pale ale. All three beers are light, refreshing, but not overwhelming.

An entree course with dark meat — ham, pork, beef — would be complemented by a more robust, assertive and darker beer — brown or Scottish ale, porter, stout.

Dessert offers the widest choice. Cheese and fruit or even cakes and cookies go wonderfully with stout, bock, lambic, or Christmas styles. The challenge in matching beers with desserts is discovering which particular beer styles, such as sweet stout or lambic, best complements flavorful desserts — ginger cookies or chocolate cake, for example.

The adventure in serving specialty beers is learning about the beers and trying them with your favorite foods. The joy is discovering the marriage of those beers and foods that suits you — and your guests.

Bon appetit!

Lindemans Kriek
Lindemans Brewery
Brabant, Belgium

CHAPTER SEVEN

HOLIDAY TRADITIONS

O ne can learn about a nation by studying its culinary customs. The rituals of eating and drinking — and the food and drink themselves — are more than an indication of the resources a nation has to devote to sustaining the population; they also reflect the national self-esteem.

A people who endeavor for variety, atmosphere, and even extravagance in eating and drinking would seem to think well of themselves. On the other hand, a nation that puts unimaginative food on the table in monotonous circumstances probably has more problems than just national wealth.

ARE WE LOSING OUR APPRECIATION FOR FOOD?

We seem to be surrendering something in America — a genuine enjoyment of food as a focus in our social lives. Fast food restaurants, franchise hamburger and taco joints, frozen foods and home-delivered pizza indicate that food is almost secondary to the convenience and speed with which it is consumed. Eating in America is sometimes more an exercise in instant gratification than an opportunity to relax and enjoy food and people in sociable surroundings.

Although the stress of everyday life may make fast food franchises a necessity, there also should be opportunities to celebrate the experience of food and drink in an atmosphere that nourishes the soul as much as it does the body.

IN AN EARLIER ERA...

In earlier times, the social customs of food and drink were a cherished part of daily life. People spent hours together eating, drinking, talking, laughing and sharing their dreams and experiences. Those earlier eras, of course, were times that did not have the present day incessant diversions of TV, movies, sports and entertainment spectacles, leisure and travel.

The Victorian Age in England was one of those eras when the ritual of food and drink occupied the best hours of the day. These times were well documented by Charles Dickens in his novels chronicling the ordinary lives of Londoners of all stations in life.

There was no lack of hardships for the people Dickens wrote about, but this didn't seem to stop them from enjoying each other's company at the public house, coaching inn, dining hall, or tavern over a plate of steaming food and a tankard of freshly brewed ale.

For the urban working class and rural poor, these inns, pubs and taverns were the only social outlets available for them to conduct daily rituals of commerce, gossip, love and treachery. When Dickens' "Pickwick Papers" appeared in 1836, there were 50,000 pubs in the country — one in every neighborhood — with polished brass, pewter tankards, frosted glass, beer engines and colorful names like The Nutmeg Grater Inn, Jolly Sailor, and Bricklayer's Arms.

English gentlemen would sit for hours in a pub or gin palace smoking their "churchwardens" (clay pipes) and drinking dark ales while eyeing the ladies. Per capita consumption of ale was more than 43 imperial gallons — not counting wine, gin, spirits and rum. The average Englishman spent more on drink in the 19th century than he did on rent.

AN ORDINARY DAY... AND NIGHT IN DICKENS' LONDON

Lunch for clerks and middle class merchants in London would be taken in "slap-bangs" or chophouses which were packed during the lunch hour and early afternoon. Conditions were noisy, crowded and austere — a sandy floor, and wooden boxes or benches to sit down on. A fire usually blazed in the corner fireplace and a large window facing the street was filled with platters of steaming roast beef and

Once inside, the hungry office workers and clerks would feast on chops, bread, cheese, pickled walnuts, kidney pie, Welsh rarebit, and steaming Yorkshire pudding. Whiskey, triple stouts, wine and cider were consumed throughout the meal or until the clerks were pushed out the door to make room for the next crowd of hungry workers.[1]

The rich merchants, bankers and solicitors had even more sumptuous feasts at nightly banquets at mansions or the numerous men's clubs around London. Beginning with a couple of soup and fish dishes, they would make their way through as many as six entrees of game and fish followed by roasts, salads, vegetables, biscuits, fondues and then dessert. All this, of course, would be washed down by bottles of sherry, ports, wines, ales and numerous toasts of special drinks before the men would adjourn to meet their ladies who were not allowed into the banquets or men's clubs.

Then, during the high social seasons, a wealthy gentleman might be invited to attend a week-long ball/supper where as many as sixty dishes would be served and liberally accompanied by desserts, wines, liqueurs, cordials and assorted mulled wines and ales.[2]

TRADITIONAL BRITISH DRINKS

The Victorians were particularly creative when it came to concocting drinks for these special occasions or to serve friends at home. They scarcely limited themselves to serving wine, gin, rum or even ale by themselves. Rather, they mixed drinks, added spices, fruits, sugar and assorted herbs, creating fragrant and highly potent drinks that they consumed by the hour!

A common procedure was to take ale or wine, fortify it with gin or rum, add sugar and spices, then heat it over an open hearth or by inserting a hot poker from the fire. They also gave these drinks colorful names — yard of flannel, dog's nose, flip, brown betty, sack, posset, negus, rumfustian, purl, and lamb's wool.

An entire class of drinks were named after the high church offices — Pope, Bishop, Cardinal, Archbishop, Beadle, Churchwarden and Chorister — made with different wine, ale, or spirit. The drinks were named by how the color matched the vestments worn by the respective cleric. For example, a Cardinal was made with red wine and spices; a Bishop with Seville oranges and ruby port.

Even old Scrooge himself, in "A Christmas Carol," imbibed in these traditional drinks. After his dream, Scrooge says he will talk about Bob Cratchit's future employment over a Christmas bowl of "smoking Bishop."

PHOTO BY MING LEONG

*A holiday tradition — enjoying Christmas
beers at the Dickens Inn, Philadelphia.*

REVIVING OLD TRADITIONS

During the winter of 1988-1989, I was presented with the opportunity
to participate in holiday banquets much like the Victorians might have
attended in the 19th century.

A feature at the dinners was the Christmas beers that are enjoying
a revival in the specialty beer revolution. Small batches of holiday beers
were traditionally brewed in Europe in the 19th century with breweries

making darker, maltier, and spicier beers with higher alcohol content and festive tastes.

The Dickens Inn in Philadelphia even invited Cedric Dickens, great-grandson of Charles, to fly over from London to serve as special guest at its dinner. The Dickens Inn is one of the establishments around the world that keeps the Dickens spirit alive by presenting English foods in a pub setting complete with authentic engravings and artifacts of the Victorian era.

Cedric was a delightful gentleman full of anecdotes about his great-grandfather and the food and drink of his times. Cedric shared a few old recipes for "bubble and squeak" and "grilled bloater" that he remembered his grandfather told him from his own childhood.

After the dinner, Cedric pronounced the Christmas beers "damn fine for British ales" and said he imagined his great-grandfather had put away many like them at similar festivities more than 100 years ago.

Christmas Ale 1988
Anchor Brewery
San Francisco, California

HOLIDAY MENUS

$$\boxed{1}$$

REAL BEER PORTFOLIO TASTING
DICKENS INN
PHILADELPHIA, PA

APPETIZER
London Peasouper
(Green Pea and Ham Soup)

BEERS
Young's Ram Rod, Aass Pilsener

ENTREE
Brewers Roast Beef & Yorkshire Pudding
with Roasted Spuds
Covent Garden Vegetable Selection
Young's Bitter (draft) Aass Bock, Dock Street

DESSERT
Rhubarb Crumble with Custard

BEERS
Young's Winter Warmer 1988, Aass Jubilee

2

CHRISTMAS BEER DINNER
WATER'S EDGE
CAPE MAY, NJ

APPETIZER
Sauteed Oysters
with Mushrooms and Leeks in Puff Pastry

BEERS
Anchor 1988 Christmas Ale

SALAD
Seasonal Green Salad with Dijon Vinaigrette

BEERS
Sierra Nevada Celebration Ale 1988
Coors Winterfest

ENTREE
Roast Loin of Pork with Dried Fruits
Madeira-Molasses Glaze
Spiced Sweet Potato Croquettes

BEERS
Young's Winter Warmer 1988, Wurzburger Hofbrau

DESSERT
Chocolate Fantasy Cake

BEERS
Samichlaus

CHEF: Neil Elshon

TRADITIONAL HOLIDAY DRINKS

England has many beer-based drinks with fascinating names and legends. Although the origins of many are lost in mythology, the drinks have survived and are featured during celebrations, particularly at Christmas, when old friends and traditions are remembered.

Some of these drinks were prescribed for medicinal purposes such as colds, headaches, or simple aches and pains. Today they make popular party time drinks for guests willing to experiment with ancient recipes and pay respects to earlier generations.

WASSAIL

"Waes hale," (loosely translated, "all hale to you") or wassail, goes back at least to medieval times when farmers would pour ale on the roots of their orchards' trees at Christmas to thank the gods for the fall harvest and as a toast to next year's crop.

In more modern times, a host would serve wassail to guests during Christmas to show respect and appreciation. Tradition and custom would determine the type of container, the spices used, and the ceremony to accompany the serving. Traditionalists insist a maple wood bowl (the farmer toasting his orchard?) is the only way wassail should be served.

6 crab or sour apples
8 tablespoons brown sugar
3 pints British ale (or 2 pints ale, 1 stout or porter)
½ teaspoon ground nutmeg
½ teaspoon cinnamon
½ teaspoon ginger
6 whole cloves
½ cup granulated sugar
1½ cup dry sherry
½ lemon sliced

Decorate serving bowl with springs of holly and Christmas ornaments. Roast apples in oven for a half hour at 350° F.

Place ale, sugar, spices, and sherry into bowl and heat on stove for 15 minutes but don't boil.

Take apples out of oven, cool, slice, and place in bottom of serving bowl. Dust with spices and add lemon slices.

Pour hot ale mixture into punch bowl and sprinkle more spices on top. Serve hot in punch glasses.

BISHOP

Bishop was a showpiece of conviviality, with its roasted Seville oranges studded with cloves. Probably introduced by Dutch sailors in the Middle ages, it was served at guild and university banquets in cut-glass bowls resembling a bishop's miter.

An entire set of ecclesiastical drinks were favorites of Victorians — Pope, Cardinal, Archbishop, Bishop, Beadle, Churchwarden and Chorister. The name of each drink was determined by the color of the clerical garb: Pope (burgundy); Cardinal (champagne or Rhine wine); Archbishop (claret or sherry); Bishop (ruby port); Churchwarden (ale, champagne, brandy with splash of port); Beadle (raisin and ginger wine or beer).

All drinks were made with Seville or tart oranges studded with a dozen cloves, grated nutmeg, sugar, lemon, and wine.

> **3 bottles dark ale or ruby port**
> **½ teaspoon grated nutmeg**
> **4 Seville or tart oranges**
> **4 tablespoons brown sugar**
> **1 lemon sliced**
> **24 whole cloves**

Spike cloves into oranges and bake in oven at 300° F for 20-30 minutes or until peels become singed.

Heat ale and sugar on stove but don't boil.

Remove oranges from oven and cut into pieces, removing seeds. Pour warm ale into punch bowl, add orange quarters and lemon slices. Serve in punch glasses with each receiving orange slice and dash of grated nutmeg.

BROWN BETTY

2 bottles ale
1 cup cognac or brandy
¼ teaspoon cinnamon
3 cloves
¼ cup brown sugar
2 cups water

Mix all ingredients in bowl and chill in refrigerator before serving in wine glasses or goblets.

DOG'S NOSE

1 pint stout
2 oz gin
1 tablespoon brown sugar
pinch nutmeg

Warm stout on a stove, add sugar and gin, sprinkle nutmeg on top and serve warm.

Other versions of this recipe use more gin and even lager.

MULLED ALE

bottle dark ale
tablespoon honey
pinch of cinnamon, nutmeg, ginger
½ pint rum or brandy

Add spices and honey to ale warmed over stove. Stir until dissolved, then add rum or brandy and serve in glass cups.

BLACK VELVET

bottle of stout
½ bottle champagne

Pour champagne and stout into punch bowl. Serve in large goblets or snifter glasses.

FLIP

2 bottles ale
3 tablespoons sugar
rind from lemon
½ teaspoon cinnamon
6 egg yolks
2 tablespoons sugar
½ teaspoon nutmeg

Place all but 1 cup ale in saucepan and heat on stove slowly.

Rub sugar on lemon rinds until sugar is "yellowed." Add sugar to ale saucepan and heat to slow boil. Remove from stove and add remaining ale.

Beat egg yolks in separate bowl, add nutmeg and two tablespoons sugar, and pour hot ale on mixture. Stir.

Return mixture to stove and heat again. Remove and pour between saucepan and bowl until foam begins to appear.

Serve in glass cups.

LAMB'S WOOL

3 bottles dark ale
6-8 crab or tart apples
3 tablespoons brown sugar
⅛ teaspoon grated nutmeg
⅛ teaspoon grated ginger

Heat ale, spices and sugar in bowl on stove.
Core and mash apples into pulp.
Add pulped apples to ale and mix hot ingredients.
Pour into pitcher or bowl and serve warm.

RECIPES AND MENUS

The following recipes and menus were designed to acquaint readers, chefs and cooks with the variety of foods that can be prepared using specialty beers.

The recipes recommend specific beer styles in cooking certain foods. This does not mean that other beer styles should not be tried. For example, most poultry and seafood recipes specify pilsener, ale and amber lager while darker meats, stews and soups call for porters and stouts.

The first time you try a recipe choose one of the recommended beers styles. When repeating the recipe try another style and compare the difference. A poultry recipe may ask for amber lager or pale ale; the second time try a wheat or steam beer.

Another suggestion is to experiment with your own recipes. Anytime a recipe calls for water, wine, milk or broth, try a beer using the guideline of lighter colored and textured beers (pilseners, pale ale, amber lager, wheat and steam beers) with lighter meats, and darker and more complex beers (porter, stout, bock, seasonal beers) with red meats and heartier fare.

Finally, any recipe recommending wine deserves to have a lambic fermentation beer tried as a substitute. With the extraordinary combination of a unique fermentation process, the use of wheat and macerated cherries or raspberries, "winey" overtones and lactic taste, lambic beers offer an exciting alternative when "ordinary" beers may seem out of place.

The objective of this book all along has been to take the mystery out of beer and beer styles and to acquaint readers with some basic recipes and menus. The first step is learning about specialty beers and trying them in standard recipes.

*If the experience proves to be a positive one
(and I'm convinced it will), a logical next step might be to
consider stocking a range of specialty beers to use in
everyday cooking. A refrigerator stocked with specialty
beers can be arranged with a little shopping and planning
— and at a fraction of the cost of building
and maintaining a wine cellar.*

*A second refrigerator in the basement — possibly used
or a compact unit — could hold dozens of specialty beers
for dinners and special occasions. But before we consider
laying down some specialty beers for the long winter
(or summer, or fall, or spring), let's try the recipes
and sample the results.*

APPETIZERS AND PARTY FOOD

Classic Beer Cheese

Recommended beer: *Dark ale, porter*

1 lb. shredded sharp Cheddar
   cheese, at room temperature
3 cloves garlic, mashed
1 TBS Worcestershire sauce
1 tsp dry mustard
2-3 dashes Tabasco sauce, or to
taste
1 c. beer
½ tsp salt, or to taste

Combine cheese, garlic, Worcestershire sauce, mustard, and Tabasco sauce in a food processor and blend until smooth. Add beer, a little at a time, until the mixture is of spreading consistency. Taste for salt and adjust if necessary.

Pack the spread into an airtight container and chill thoroughly. Serve at room temperature.

Beer to serve: Brown ale or pale ale, porter

Beer and Cheese Fondue

Recommended beer: *Amber lager or ale*

1½ c. beer
½ lb. Swiss cheese
¼ lb. Cheddar cheese
¼ lb. Monterey Jack cheese

Heat the beer until just before boiling in a chafing dish over hot water. Shred or cube the cheeses and add them gradually to the beer, stirring until all the cheese has melted.

1 TBS corn starch
2 TBS water
1 tsp salt
¼ tsp white pepper
⅛ tsp nutmeg

In a small bowl, combine the corn starch and water, stirring until smooth. Add salt, pepper, and nutmeg, and then pour this mixture into the fondue, stirring constantly. Cook and stir until the fondue is smooth and thick.

Serve the fondue with cubes of crusty French bread for dipping. Firm vegetables, such as broccoli, cauliflower, or zucchini are untraditional, but delicious, when dipped into this fondue.

Beer to serve: Pale ale

Baked Crabmeat Appetizer

Recommended beer: *Ale*

1 1 lb. round loaf rye bread

Preheat the oven to 300 degrees.

Slice the top off of the loaf and scoop out the center, leaving about a 1″ thick shell. Cut the soft bread into cubes. Set them aside in a plastic bag.

12 oz. lump crabmeat, carefully picked over
2 8 oz. packages cream cheese, at room temperature
2 TBS grated green onion or fresh chives
2 TBS beer
1 tsp lemon juice
½ tsp Worcestershire sauce
1 dash hot pepper sauce
¼ tsp salt

Combine all ingredients in a large bowl. Mix thoroughly and taste for seasoning. Adjust for salt or hot pepper sauce, as necessary.

Fill the bread shell with the crabmeat mixture. Replace the top. Wrap completely in foil and place on a baking sheet. Bake for 1½ to 2 hours. Unwrap and remove the top. Serve hot, with reserved bread cubes for dipping.

Beer to serve: Pale ale or amber lager

Clam and Parmesan Appetizers

Recommended beer: *Ale*

¼ c. butter, melted
½ c. breadcrumbs
¼ c. beer
2 TBS grated Parmesan cheese
4 cloves garlic, minced
1 TBS fresh parsley, minced
1 tsp oregano
½ tsp dried rosemary
¼ tsp dried basil

Preheat oven to 375 degrees.

Blend all ingredients together until smooth.

1 10 ½ oz. can minced clams
salt
pepper

Drain clams, reserving liquid. Add clams to seasoning mixture, using as much of the reserved clam juice as necessary to achieve a mixture with the texture of oatmeal. Add salt and pepper to taste.

36 rounds of melba toast

Spoon clam mixture evenly onto toast rounds.

Place appetizers on a greased baking sheet and bake for about 10 minutes, until they are lightly browned. Serve hot.

Beer to serve: Ale, bock

Beer Batter Onion Rings

Recommended beer: *Amber lager, pilsener, pale ale*

6 oz. flour
1 tsp salt
2 eggs separated
8 oz. beer
2 TBS vegetable oil
3-4 large onions
pinch pepper

Sift flour, salt, pepper into bowl. Whisk egg yolks, beer, oil and add to flour mixture. Stir until smooth, set aside. Slice onions, not too small. Beat egg whites until stiff.

After flour and beer mixture has stood for half hour, fold egg whites into batter.

Dip onion rings and fry on both sides in hot fat fryer heated to 375 degrees.

Remove when both sides are browned or after about two minutes.

These onion rings are light, tasty and delicious. If planning a party for more than 6 people, you might want to double the recipe.

Beer to serve: Amber lager, ale.

Beer-Cheese Dip for Vegetables

Recommended beer: *Amber lager, pale pilsener*

**2 c. shredded Cheddar cheese,
  at room temperature**
**2 oz. cream cheese, at room
  temperature**
¼ tsp dry mustard
1 clove garlic, mashed
**2-4 dashes Tabasco sauce,
  to taste**
⅛ tsp Worcestershire sauce
dash paprika
½ c. beer
salt, to taste

Combine cheese, mustard, garlic, Tabasco, and Worcestershire sauce in a food processor. Process 30 seconds to blend. With the processor running, add the beer gradually, blending until the mixture is smooth. Taste for salt, and adjust if necessary.

Transfer the mixture to a serving bowl and chill an hour or more to allow the flavors to blend. Bring to room temperature before serving. Garnish with fresh parsley and paprika. Serve with raw vegetables.

Beer to serve: Light lager

SALADS AND VEGETABLES

Southwest Salad

Recommended beer: *Brown ale or pale ale*

1 10½ oz. can tomato soup
¾ c. vegetable oil
½ c. beer
¼ tsp dry mustard
1 tsp salt
1 tsp sugar
1 tsp horseradish
1 tsp Worcestershire sauce
1 small onion
1 clove garlic, mashed
¾ tsp white pepper
½ tsp chili powder
5 drops Tabasco sauce

Mince the onion in a blender or food processor. Add the remaining ingredients and blend thoroughly. Chill at least one hour before using.

Pour over mixed greens: iceberg, red leaf, Boston, Romaine lettuce, spinach, kale, etc., combined with kidney and/or garbanzo beans, diced avocado, green and red bell peppers, black olives, tomato wedges.

Beer to serve: Light lager, ale, porter

Spicy Cold Shrimp Salad

Recommended beer: *Pale ale*

3 TBS butter
1 TBS olive oil
4 cloves garlic, mashed

Melt the butter and oil in a skillet. Add the garlic and saute over medium low heat for about 1 minute.

1 tsp Worcestershire sauce
½ tsp salt
½ tsp thyme
½ tsp oregano
⅛ tsp crushed red pepper
1 c. beer

Blend in seasonings and add beer. Cover and cook for 2 minutes.

1 lb. fresh shrimp, shelled
and deveined

Add shrimp. Cover pan and cook until shrimp are pink and opaque, 4-5 minutes. Remove from heat, drain shrimp, and discard cooking liquid.

juice of 1 lemon

Toss the shrimp with the lemon juice. Chill thoroughly.

Serve the shrimp on a bed of lettuce — Boston is a good choice. Garnish with dill pickles, black olives, and green onions.

Beer to serve: Amber lager, pale ale

Cole Slaw with Beer Dressing

Recommended beer: *Pale ale or pilsener*

Dressing:
1/3 **c. beer**
1/2 **c. mayonnaise**
1/4 **c. sour cream**
1/2 **tsp celery seed**
1/4 **tsp ground coriander**
1/8 **tsp Tabasco sauce**
salt and pepper to taste

Combine all dressing ingredients and blend well.

2 **lb. cabbage, shredded**
2 **medium carrots, shredded**

Toss cabbage and carrots together. Pour dressing over the slaw and toss to blend. Chill 1 hour before serving.

Beer to serve: Ale, pilsener

Hot and Spicy Refried Beans

Recommended beer: *Amber lager, ale*

**1 c. pinto or kidney beans,
  soaked overnight and drained**
½ TBS baking soda

Place the beans in a large, deep pot and add enough water to cover them by 1". Bring to a boil and cook for 15 minutes. Reduce the heat and sprinkle the baking soda over the beans. Stir until foam rises to the top of the pot, about 1 minute. Drain the beans in a colander and rinse.

1 small onion, chopped
2 garlic cloves, mashed
2 slices bacon, diced

Return the beans to the pot. Add the onion, garlic, and bacon. Add water to cover the beans by about 2". Cover and cook over low heat for 2 hours.

2 c. beer
½ tsp sugar
½ TBS chili powder
½ TBS ground cumin
1 tsp oregano

Remove 2 cups liquid from the pot. Add the beer, sugar, and spices. Cover and cook 45 minutes. Drain well.

¼ c. bacon drippings
1 small onion, chopped
1 clove garlic, mashed
¼-½ c. beer
salt, to taste

In a large, heavy skillet, melt the bacon drippings over medium heat. Saute the onion and garlic. Add the beans, a little at a time, mashing and stirring with a potato masher after each addition. Add beer as needed if beans become too dry. Salt to taste.

Beer to serve: Amber lager, ale

Hot German Potato Salad

Recommended beer: *Amber lager, pale ale*

2 lbs. potatoes

Peel, slice and boil potatoes; set aside.

4 strips bacon
1 cup chopped celery
½ chopped onion
1 TBS salt
1 TBS butter
2 TBS breadcrumbs
1 tsp dry mustard
1 tsp sugar
1 tsp Tabasco sauce
½ bottle lager

Grill bacon, crumble. Saute onions, celery in large saucepan, add salt. Blend in breadcrumbs, mustard, sugar and stir.

Heat beer and Tabasco to boil while stirring. Remove from heat.

2 TBS chopped parsley

Pour beer sauce over warm potatoes, add bacon, onions, celery mixture and add parsley.

Let salad cool a half hour and serve warm as summer side dish.

Beer to serve: Amber lager, pale ale

BREADS

Classic Beer Bread

Recommended beer: *Pilsener, amber lager*

1½ c. beer 1 envelope dry yeast 1½ c. all-purpose flour	Heat beer to lukewarm over low heat. Stir in yeast until dissolved. Add flour and beat until smooth. Cover with a towel and let rise until double in bulk.
2 c. flour ½ tsp sugar tsp salt	Add flour, sugar, and salt. Turn onto floured surface and knead 5 to 8 minutes, until dough is smooth and elastic.

Grease a large bowl and set the dough in it, turning to coat all surfaces of the dough. Cover and let rise until double in bulk, about 1 hour. Punch down the dough, brush the top with oil, cover and let rise again.

Shape the dough into a loaf and place in a greased 5x8″ pan. Let rise.

Bake at 375 degrees 45 to 55 minutes, until the loaf sounds hollow when tapped. Cool on its side on a rack before slicing.

Beer to serve: Pale ale

Rye Bread with Beer

Recommended beer: *Pale ale or brown ale*

1 c. beer
1 TBS sugar
1 envelope dry yeast

Bring the beer to a boil in a deep saucepan; lower the heat and simmer 5 minutes. Pour into a large bowl. Stir in the sugar and let cool slightly. Sprinkle on the yeast; let stand for 5 minutes, or until the yeast is foamy.

1 c. all-purpose flour
1 TBS honey
½ TBS vegetable oil
½ TBS salt
1 c. rye flour
caraway seeds

Using a wire whisk, stir in flour and honey until smooth. Add oil, salt, and caraway. Beat well. Add rye flour and beat until smooth.

½ to 1 c. all-purpose flour

Add ½ cup flour, mixing with a wooden spoon or your hands. Add more flour gradually, until the dough begins to leave the sides of the bowl. Knead in the bowl for one minute.

Turn the dough onto a lightly floured surface and knead 8 to 10 minutes, adding as little flour as necessary. Place dough into an oiled bowl, turning to coat all over. Cover and let rise until doubled in bulk, about an hour.

Turn out the dough onto a lighly floured surface and knead 2 minutes. Shape into a long, narrow loaf. Grease a baking sheet and sprinkle with corn meal. Place the loaf on the baking sheet and cover with a towel or waxed paper. Let rise until doubled in bulk, about 45 minutes.

Bake at 375 degrees for 25 to 30 minutes, until the loaf sounds hollow when tapped. Cool on a rack before slicing.

Beer to serve: Pale ale or brown ale

Whole Wheat Rolls

Whole wheat bread doesn't have to be heavy, and it doesn't have to be a chore to make. This recipe is quickly and smoothly mixed and kneaded in a food processor.

Recommended beer: *Pale ale or brown ale*

1 envelope dry yeast
c. very warm water
1 TBS light brown sugar,
  firmly packed

Sprinkle yeast into water; add ¼ c. very warm water. Add sugar and let stand until foamy, 5 to 10 minutes.

1½ c. bread flour
1½ c. whole wheat flour
2 TBS nonfat dry milk OR
  buttermilk powder
2 TBS vegetable oil
1½ tsp salt

Combine flours, milk powder, oil, and salt in food processor work bowl. Add yeast mixture. Turn on and add beer. Process until the dough cleans the sides of the work bowl.

Process until the dough is smooth and elastic, about 40 seconds. If the dough is too sticky, add more bread flour, about 1 tablespoon at a time, mixing in each addition thoroughly. If the dough is too dry, add water, 1 teaspoon at a time, again mixing thoroughly after each addition.

Place the dough in a large, oiled bowl, turning to coat entire surface. Cover with oiled plastic wrap and let rise until doubled in bulk, about 1 hour.

Punch down the dough and knead gently 1 or 2 minutes. Shape into balls about 2″ in diameter. Lightly grease a baking sheet and sprinkle with cornmeal. Place rolls on baking sheet, with sides just barely touching. Cover with towel and let rise until doubled in bulk, about 45 minutes.

Brush with a glaze made of 1 egg mixed with 1 tablespoon of water. Bake at 400 degrees for about 25 minutes, or until rolls sound hollow when tapped.

Beer to serve: Brown ale

Hearty Breakfast Bread

Easy to make, slightly sweet, with a hearty texture, this bread is delicious right from the oven on a cool morning.

Recommended beer: *Pale ale*

3 c. flour
1½ tsp baking powder
½ tsp baking soda
½ tsp salt
¼ c. brown sugar

Preheat the oven to 375 degrees. Grease a 9"x5" loaf pan.

Stir all the dry ingredients together in a large bowl.

1 12 oz. can of beer, at
  room temperature
1 egg

Pour in beer. Add egg and stir until thoroughly mixed, about 50 strokes.

Pour batter into greased loaf pan. Bake for about an hour, until the bread is a deep golden brown and sounds hollow when tapped. Remove from the pan and cool on wire rack.

Beer to serve: Ale, pilsener, amber lager

Herb Bread

Recommended beer: *Amber lager*

3 c. self-rising flour 2 TBS sugar 1 tsp ground sage ½ tsp crushed sweet basil 12 oz. beer	Combine all ingredients. Pour into a greased 9x5" baking pan.
2 TBS butter, melted	Brush the top of the batter with melted butter. Bake for 1 hour.

Remove the bread from the pan and cool on a wire rack.

Variations: Instead of sage and basil, substitute ½ tsp celery seed and 1 tsp poultry seasoning, or 1 tsp sage and 3 tsp caraway seeds.

Beer to serve: Ale, porter

Skillet Bread

The cooking method is a bit unconventional, but the result is delightful — a moist and tender bread with a light flavor. Great with chili!

Recommended beer: *Amber lager, pilsener*

4 c. baking mix 1 tsp brown sugar 2 tsp sugar 1 12 oz. bottle of beer	Combine ingredients and stir until thoroughly blended.

Pour into a well-greased 12" iron skillet* and cover. Cook over low heat on top of the stove for 35 to 40 minutes. Test by inserting a toothpick or thin knife into the center; bread is done if toothpick comes out clean. Serve hot, sliced into wedges.

*You can use a 10" iron skillet instead, but it must have a higher-domed cover, since the bread will rise higher.

Beer to serve: Pale ale

Cheddar Muffins

These muffins are crusty on the outside and tender and moist on the inside.

Recommended beer: *Amber lager, pilsener*

2 c. flour   Preheat oven to 400 degrees.
2 TBS sugar
1 TBS baking powder   Sift dry ingredients together.
¼ tsp dry mustard

1 c. beer   Stir together beer, oil, and egg.
¼ c. oil   Add cheese.
1 egg, beaten
1¼ c. grated cheddar cheese

Stir dry ingredients into beer mixture. Spoon batter into muffin pan, filling each cup one-half to two-thirds full. Bake until golden brown and crusty, about 20 to 25 minutes. Cool in pan for 5 minutes, then turn muffins onto wire rack to finish cooling.

Beer to serve: Pale ale

Pancakes

Pancakes made with beer have a mildly tangy flavor and a light texture.

Recommended beer: *Ale*

1½ c. sifted flour **½ tsp salt** **½ TBS baking powder** **½ TBS sugar**	Measure dry ingredients into a large bowl.
1 egg **⅔ c. beer** **¾ c. milk** **2 TBS melted butter**	Add egg, beer, and milk. Beat with an electric mixer at medium speed until batter is light and frothy; batter will be the consistency of cream. Blend in butter.

Cook the pancakes on a hot griddle, lightly greased.

If you measure the batter onto the griddle using a soup ladle, you will have about 18 pancakes.

Beer to serve: Ale

Beer Waffles

Recommended beer: *Amber lager, pilsener*

3 c. beer
2 eggs
½ c. vegetable oil
½ tsp salt
3½ c. flour
½ tsp dried thyme, optional
½ tsp dried sage, optional

Combine the beer, eggs, and oil in a large mixing bowl. Beat with a wire whisk or electric mixer on low speed until smooth. Add dry ingredients and beat again until smooth.

Let the batter stand at room temperature for 1-2 hours. Beat lightly again. Cook on a well-oiled waffle iron.

These are very substantial waffles, and they stand up well to all the fixings of a hearty country breakfast. Try topping them with creamed eggs or chicken for a simple Saturday night supper.

Beer to serve: Dark ale, porter, sweet stout

Beer Syrup

Try this on your waffles and pancakes next time.

Recommended beer: *Ale, porter, sweet stout*

1 bottle beer
3 c. brown sugar
1 oz. butter (optional)

Heat sugar and beer in saucepan until it starts to boil. (Add butter). Stir until sugar is dissolved.

Pour over waffles or pancakes and keep warm.

Beer to serve: Porter, stout

POULTRY

Beer-Marinated Baked Chicken Wings

Recommended beer: *Ale, wheat beer, amber lager, steam beer*

Marinade:

¼ c. olive oil
½ c. beer
¼ c. soy sauce
⅛ c. lemon juice
½ tsp. salt
¼ tsp. pepper
⅛ tsp. ginger
1 clove garlic, mashed

3 to 3½ lbs. chicken wings

Combine all ingredients and blend well.

Rinse the chicken well under very cold water. Drain on paper towels. Place the chicken in a large bowl or plastic bag and pour the marinade over it. Turn all the pieces to coat thoroughly with marinade. Cover tightly and refrigerate 24 hours.

Preheat the oven to 350 degrees. Place chicken, skin-side up, in a roasting pan. Bake until the chicken is a deep golden brown, about 1 hour.

Beer to serve: Ale, steam beer, wheat beer, amber lager

Chicken Baked In Beer

Recommended beer: *Amber lager, pale ale, pilsener*

Preheat oven to 400 degrees.

1 frying chicken, 3 to 3½ lbs.
2 TBS olive oil

Rinse the chicken under cold water; drain and dry with paper towels. Rub with olive oil.

2 TBS butter
2 medium carrots, sliced
1 celery stalk, sliced
1 medium onion, chopped
2 slices bacon, diced

Melt butter in a Dutch oven over medium low heat. Add vegetables and bacon and cook until vegetables are limp and bacon is lightly crisped. Remove vegetables. Increase heat to medium high and brown the chicken on all sides, turning carefully to avoid tearing the skin. Return vegetables to the pot.

¼ tsp marjoram
1¼ c. beer

Sprinkle chicken and vegetables with marjoram. Add beer. Roast, uncovered, about 45 minutes, until the chicken is tender and juices run clear.

1 TBS lemon juice
salt
pepper

Remove chicken to a warm platter. Place Dutch oven on top of the stove, over medium heat. Skim off some of the fat and cook until juices are reduced slightly, about 10 minutes. Stir in lemon juice; season with salt and pepper to taste.

Carve the chicken. Spoon a little of the gravy over each serving; pass the rest separately. Serve with a lightly steamed green vegetable and rice.

Beer to serve: Ale, amber lager

Barbecued Chicken

This is a sweet barbecue sauce, with a hint of spiciness.

Recommended beer: *Amber lager, steam beer*

1 frying chicken, cut into serving pieces
12 oz. beer

Place chicken in a large bowl. Pour beer over chicken, cover, and marinate for 2 hours.

Sauce:

12 oz. beer
½ c. catsup
½ c. onion, finely chopped
¼ c. mushrooms, finely chopped
2 cloves garlic, mashed
½ TBS Worcestershire sauce
1 TBS lemon juice
½ tsp lemon peel
1 tsp chili powder
2 tsp paprika
2 tsp dry mustard
1 tsp salt
1 TBS coffee
2 TBS brown sugar

Combine all sauce ingredients in a 1½ quart saucepan. Cook over low heat until thickened, about 45 minutes.

Drain the chicken and place, skin-side down, on a hot, oiled grill. Brown the chicken on all sides, then baste with the sauce, turning and basting frequently until the chicken is done, about 40 minutes total cooking time.

Beer to serve: Steam beer, pale ale, amber lager

Spanish Chicken With Rice

*Beer gives this dish a smooth and mellow flavor;
saffron gives it a sunny glow.*

Recommended beer: *Ale, steam beer, amber lager*

2 TBS olive oil
**3 lb. frying chicken, cut into
   serving pieces**

Heat the oil in a large, heavy skillet over medium heat. Brown the chicken on all sides. Remove from the pan.

1 large onion, chopped
1 medium green pepper, chopped
2 cloves garlic, mashed

Saute the onion, pepper, and garlic in the remaining oil. Return the chicken to the pan.

1 15 oz. can tomatoes, drained
1 c. chicken broth
1 c. beer
2 bay leaves
1 tsp salt
generous pinch saffron

Add the tomatoes, broth, beer, bay leaves, salt, and saffron to the skillet. Cover, reduce the heat to low, and cook for 20 minutes.

1 c. long grained rice

Add the rice and stir gently, to distribute evenly through the chicken and vegetables. Cover and cook 20 minutes.

1 c. zucchini, diced

Add the zucchini, stir two or three times, and cook 5 to 10 minutes longer, until the zucchini is barely tender.

A salad and crisp beer bread will make this a complete meal.

Beer to serve: Amber lager, steam beer, ale

Southern-Style Fried Chicken Breasts With Beer Gravy

Recommended beer: *Amber lager or pale ale*

½ c. flour
½ tsp pepper
½ tsp salt
6 boneless chicken breasts
3 TBS vegetable oil

Combine flour, pepper, and salt in a plastic bag. Add chicken, one piece at a time, and shake bag to coat thoroughly. Reserve unused flour. Heat oil in a large, heavy skillet over medium heat and fry the chicken until crispy and golden brown on all sides. Remove chicken and drain on paper towels.

2 TBS reserved seasoned flour
1 c. milk
⅔ c. beer
⅓ c. water

Add the reserved flour to the pan drippings and stir until smooth. Gradually add milk, then beer, stirring constantly until the gravy is smooth and thick. Adjust the consistency with the water, if necessary.

Arrange the chicken on a warm serving platter and ladle the gravy over the top. Garnish with fresh parsley and toasted, slivered almonds, if desired.

Beer to serve: Amber lager, pale ale

PORK

Fresh Ham Braised in Stout

The quality of just a few ingredients makes this very simple dish a winner.

Recommended beer: *Porter, stout*

1 4 or 5 pound fresh ham
2 TBS vegetable oil

Remove skin from ham. Heat oil over medium heat in a Dutch oven. Brown ham on all sides and remove to a plate.

1 large onion, sliced
1 tsp salt, or to taste
½ tsp pepper, or to taste
1 12 oz. bottle stout

Saute onion over medium heat until limp. Sprinkle with salt and pepper. Put ham back in Dutch oven. Add stout.

Cover and bring to a boil. Reduce heat to low and cook until ham is tender, about 2 hours. Remove ham to a warm platter; thicken pan juices for gravy if desired.

Beer to serve: Dark ale, porter, stout, bock

Don't overwhelm this dish with accompaniments — boiled potatoes tossed with butter, garlic, and rosemary, a fresh green vegetable, perhaps some crisp rolls, will best complement the flavor of the meat.

Beer-Glazed Ham

Recommended beer: *Ale, porter*

1 5 lb. smoked ham
1¼ c. brown sugar
1 tsp ground cloves
½ TBS dry mustard
¼ c. beer

Preheat oven to 350 dgreees

Remove any rind from the ham and score the fat. Place the ham in a baking pan. Make a paste of the brown sugar, cloves, mustard, and beer, and rub it into the ham. Place ham in the oven.

1½ c. beer

Cook ham for about 1 hour. Baste with beer every 15-20 minutes, until the ham is a very deep golden brown.

Beer to serve: Ale, porter

Italian Sausages and Beer Casserole

Recommended beer: *Ale or bock*

2-3 lb. sweet or hot Italian
  sausages
1 large onion, sliced
½ c. mushrooms, sliced
1 14 oz. can kidney beans,
  drained
1 16 oz. can tomatoes, drained
1½ c. beer

Place all ingredients in a crock pot. Cover and cook on low heat 10 to 12 hours.

Beer to serve: Ale or porter

Spareribs in Beer

Recommended beer: *Ale, porter*

Marinade:
12 oz. beer
½ c. honey
2 TBS lemon juice
2 tsp salt
2 tsp dry mustard
¼ tsp pepper
1 tsp ginger
1 tsp ground coriander

Combine marinade ingredients in a jar and shake well, being sure that seasonings are well-blended.

5-6 lb. pork spareribs

Trim ribs and cut them apart. Place the ribs in a large bowl or baking dish. Cover with marinade and refrigerate 4 to 24 hours.

Preheat oven to 350 degrees. Use a broiling pan and its rack, or place a large wire rack over a 2″ deep baking pan.

Pour 2 cups water into the baking pan and place the rack on top. Arrange the ribs, meaty side up, on the rack. Reserve the marinade for basting. Bake for 25 minutes.

Baste the ribs, turn them over, and baste again. Bake for another 25 minutes.

Raise the oven temperature to 450 degrees. Repeat the basting and turning procedure and bake for 10 minutes longer. Remove from the oven and serve.

Beer to serve: Ale, porter, bock

Grilled Spiced Pork Chops

Marinating meat is usually praised as a way of tenderizing meat while imparting flavor. But it is also a wonderful time-saver, since most marinades take only a few minutes to prepare, and marinating time can be adjusted for almost any schedule.

Recommended beer: *Steam beer, ale*

Marinade:

¾ c. beer
¼ tsp salt
½ TBS dry mustard
½ tsp ground cloves
1½ TBS soy sauce
1 TBS honey
1 TBS marmalade
1 clove garlic, mashed
⅛ tsp Tabasco sauce

Mix marinade ingredients together thoroughly. Place the chops in a large, shallow bowl and pour the marinade over them. Cover tightly and marinate in the refrigerator at least 2 hours (or overnight).

8 loin pork chops, about 1″ thick

Place marinated chops on a well-oiled grill, 4-6 inches from the heat. Cook about 15 minutes. Baste the chops with marinade, turn and baste again. Cook until done, 15 to 20 minutes more.

Beer to serve: Ale, steam beer, amber lager

These chops can also be baked at 350 degrees, cooking about 25 minutes on each side.

BEEF

Irish Pot Roast

Recommended beer: *Porter or stout*

2 TBS vegetable oil
2 medium onions, thickly sliced

Heat oil in a heavy skillet or Dutch oven over medium heat. Add onions and cook until lightly browned. Remove to a warm dish.

2 TBS flour
1 tsp dry mustard
1 tsp salt
½ tsp pepper
3-4 pound chuck roast
tsp dried thyme
¾ c. beer

Mix together flour, mustard, salt, and pepper. Transfer to a large platter. Dredge meat in seasoned flour. Brown the meat in the oil. Add reserved onions, thyme, and beer.

Cover pan and reduce heat to low. Cook until tender, 1½ hours, turning the meat once or twice during cooking. Check seasonings and adjust for salt and pepper, to taste.

Beer to serve: Brown ale

Since this is Irish, potatoes are the obvious choice for a side dish. Steamed, buttered carrots are also a good choice.

Beer-Marinated Steak

Recommended beer: *Amber lager, ale, porter*

Marinade:

1 small onion, chopped
1 clove garlic, mashed
⅛ c. vegetable oil
1 c. beer
¾ c. chili sauce
½ TBS Worcestershire sauce
½ tsp salt

Combine all marinade ingredients in a jar and shake well.

4 8 oz. boneless sirloin steaks

Place steaks in a large, shallow dish. Cover with marinade. Refrigerate 4 to 6 hours.

Preheat broiler or grill. Cook steaks to desired doneness — about 5 minutes on a side for medium rare. Baste with marinade before and after turning.

Beer to serve: Amber lager, ale, porter

Beef Brisket and Smoked Sausages in Dark Beer

Recommended beer: *Porter or stout*

1 4 lb. beef brisket
2 lb. smoked sausages
1 medium onion, sliced
1 16 oz. can tomatoes, drained
2 medium potatoes, peeled
   and sliced
2 bay leaves
1½ c. beer

Place all ingredients in a crock pot. Cover and cook on low heat 10 hours.

Beer to serve: Ale, porter

Scandinavian Beef Stew

Recommended beer: *Ale, bock, porter, stout*

4 lb. chuck roast, cut into 2" cubes

Combine marinade ingredients in a large glass bowl. Add meat and toss to coat thoroughly. Cover tightly and refrigerate up to 3 days.

Marinade:
1 c. beer
½ c. cider vinegar
2 tsp pepper
1 tsp ground allspice
2 bay leaves
1 tsp ground thyme
2 medium onions, sliced
2 medium carrots, sliced

When ready to cook, remove meat from marinade and pat dry on paper towels. Reserve marinade.

2 TBS vegetable oil
reserved marinade

Heat the oil in a heavy skillet or Dutch oven over medium heat. Brown meat on all sides. Add 1 cup of marinade. Turn heat to low, cover, and cook about 2 hours, until meat is very tender. Add reserved marinade, if necessary, to keep meat moist.

1½ tsp corn starch
1 TBS water
¼ c. cream

Mix corn starch and water together to make a smooth paste. Remove meat to a serving dish with a slotted spoon. Stir corn starch mixture into pan gravy. Bring to a boil over medium high heat, stirring constantly, until gravy is thickened. Add cream and blend well. Pour over meat.

The traditional garnish for this stew is sour gherkins. Serve with boiled potatoes.

Beer to serve: Ale, bock, porter, stout

Beef Stew in Lager

Recommended beer: *Porter, stout, bock*

5 lb. beef chuck, cut into 2" cubes
½ c. flour, seasoned with salt and pepper
3 TBS vegetable oil

Dry beef on paper towels. Dredge beef in seasoned flour. Heat oil in Dutch oven over medium heat. Brown meat on all sides; remove to warm platter.

4 slices bacon, diced
2 medium onions, sliced
2 cloves garlic, mashed
1 c. chopped celery, stalks and leaves
3 medium carrots, sliced

Saute bacon in same pot until almost crisp. Add vegetables and cook over medium heat until onions are limp and golden, about 15 minutes. Return meat to pot.

1 tsp dried thyme
1 tsp oregano
2 bay leaves
1½ c. beer
1 tsp salt
½ tsp pepper

Add thyme, oregano, bay leaves, beer, salt, and pepper to stew. Cover and cook over low heat until meat is tender, about 2½ hours. Stir occasionally and taste for salt and pepper.

Serve the stew with egg noodles or boiled or mashed potatoes, with a crisp salad and crusty bread.

Beer to serve: Ale, porter or stout

All American Chili

Recommended beer: *Amber lager, pale ale*

2 lbs. dried kidney beans
2 lbs. ground chuck
1 large onion, diced
1 green pepper, chopped
½ c. chopped celery stalks
1 TBS salt

Soak beans overnight in covered pot. The next morning simmer beans with salt until beans are tender, keeping pot covered.

Brown beef and onion in skillet, pour off fat.

¼ c. sugar
3 cloves garlic
3 TBS chili powder
1 TBS dry mustard
2 bottles beer

Add sugar, chili powder, garlic, mustard to beef with one bottle beer. Cover and simmer 30 minutes.

2 6-oz. cans tomato paste

Add tomato paste to beans and stir. Add beef, celery, peppers and beans together into large pot and simmer 30 minutes adding remaining bottle of beer.

Cheddar muffins or herb bread are excellent complements to this chili.

Beer to serve: Amber lager, bock, wheat or steam beer

Beer Hamburgers

Recommended beer: *Amber lager*

1½ lbs. ground beef
1 medium onion, chopped
½ c. seasoned breadcrumbs
¼ c. grated parmesan cheese
1 tsp steak sauce
½ tsp seasoning salt
½ tsp ground pepper
1 c. beer

Mix hamburger in bowl with chopped onion, breadcrumbs, steak sauce, salt, pepper, and splash of beer. Shape into round patties for cooking.

Make small hole in top of each hamburger patty and pour in approximately 1 oz. of beer.

Let stand 2-3 minutes for beer to absorb into meat; add to frying pan.

When meat is cooked on one side, close "hole" with fork and turn meat. Cook for five more minutes.

The beer will have soaked through hamburger by the time it is turned on second side.

Beer to serve: Amber lager in summer, ale, bock in fall or spring.

FISH

Trout in Beer

Recommended beer: *Pilsener, amber lager, ale*

3 fresh trout
1 c. beer
1 c. dry white wine
½ c. vinegar

Wash and clean trout, place in saucepan. Mix beer, wine, vinegar and pour over fish in saucepan.

Heat mixture to boil, turn down heat and simmer 10-15 minutes, turning fish over.

1 lemon, half in slices

Remove fish, squeeze lemon over fish, garnish with lemon slices and parsley.

Beer to serve: Pilsener, amber lager, ale

Shrimp in Beer

Recommended beer: *Amber lager, pale ale*

1 lb. shrimp
1 bottle beer
1 lemon, squeezed
2 bay leaves
1 c. water

Place beer, water, shrimp, bay leaves and lemon juice in pan and bring to boil.

¼ tsp. thyme
2 red peppers
4 sprigs fresh dill
¼ c. celery leaves

Add spices, dill, peppers, celery and simmer covered for five minutes.

Remove from heat and let cool. De-vein and chill for 1 hour.

Serve in bowls over bed of crisp lettuce, lemons and cocktail sauce.

Beer to serve: Amber lager, pale ale

Crispy Catfish

Recommended beer: *Pilsener, amber lager*

6 filets catfish (or other light fish)
1 c. buttermilk
1 egg, beaten
1 bottle beer

Clean fish, place in bowl with beer, cover and set in refrigerator 30 minutes.

½ c. flour
¼ tsp salt
¼ tsp pepper
1½ c. cornmeal

In four separate bowls put:

1) ½ c. buttermilk
2) beaten egg and remaining buttermilk
3) flour, salt, pepper
4) cornmeal

Dip fish in each bowl in order ending with cornmeal.

Put fish pieces into deep fat fryer heated to 375 degrees two at a time; fry 6 to 8 minutes or until golden brown.

Remove, drain, and serve warm.

Beer to serve: Amber lager, ale, bock

DESSERTS

Tea Bread with Stout

Recommended beer: *Stout*

1 c. butter 1 c. firmly packed brown sugar grated peel of 1 lemon	Preheat the oven to 325 degrees. Grease a 9x5″ loaf pan. Cream butter, sugar, and lemon peel until light and fluffy.
3 ½ c. flour ½ tsp salt ½ tsp baking soda ½ tsp allspice 4 eggs, beaten	Sift together dry ingredients, and add to creamed butter and sugar alternately with eggs, beating well after each addition.
1 c. raisins 1 c. currants 1 c. chopped walnuts 3 TBS stout	Fold in raisins, currants, and nuts. Stir in stout.

Pour batter into prepared loaf pan. Bake 1 hour. Reduce heat to 300 degrees and bake until cake is done, and a toothpick inserted into the center comes out clean, about 1 hour. Cool 10-15 minutes on wire rack, then remove from pan.

Serve with sweet butter, cream cheese, or preserves.

Beer to serve: Stout, lambic beer

Brown Sugar Cake

This is a big cake, very moist, with an even texture and a nutty flavor.

Recommended beer: *Ale or bock*

3 c. flour
1 ½ TBS baking powder
1 ½ tsp salt
½ tsp cinnamon
½ tsp allspice
¼ tsp mace

Preheat the oven to 350 degrees. Grease and flour 10″ tube pan.

Sift together dry ingredients.

½ c. soft butter or margarine
1 c. brown sugar
4 eggs, separated

Cream butter and sugar until light and fluffy. Add egg yolks and beat well.

In a separate bowl, beat egg whites until stiff, but not dry.

12 oz. beer

Add to butter, sugar, and eggs alternately with dry ingredients — batter will be stiff. Gently fold in beaten egg whites.

Pour the batter into prepared cake pan. Bake for about 1 hour, until cake is golden brown and a toothpick inserted into the center comes out clean. Cool in pan 10 minutes, remove from pan and cool completely on a wire rack. Glaze with brown sugar glaze.

Fill the center of the cake with fresh fruit, or serve with ice cream.

Beer to serve: Ale or Porter

Brown Sugar Glaze

¼ c. butter
1 c. sifted confectioners' sugar
1 tsp vanilla
2 TBS hot milk

Melt butter over low heat until it just begins to brown. Remove from heat and beat in sugar and vanilla. Add enough milk to thin to desired consistency. Drizzle over cooled cake.

Custard Sauce with Beer

Recommended beer: *Bock*

3 egg yolks
1 egg
²/₃ c. flat beer
1 TBS lemon juice
½ tsp cinnamon

Combine all ingredients in top of a double boiler over gently simmering water. Beat with electric mixer at low speed. When mixture begins to thicken, increase speed and continue to beat until sauce is consistency of a soft meringue.

Serve in a heated bowl.

This is a lovely sauce for gingerbread or apple cake,

Beer to serve: Bock, stout, lambic

Gingerbread Cake

Recommended beer: *Porter, stout, bock*

½ bottle beer
¼ c. butter
½ c. brown sugar

Melt butter in 9 in. pan and sprinkle brown sugar over bottom and sides.

1½ c. crushed pineapple
1 14½ oz. package gingerbread
   mix

Pour pineapple into pan. In separate bowl put gingerbread mix and add beer. Beat until blended, spoon into pan.

confectioners sugar
ice cream

Bake in preheated oven at 350 degrees for 45 minutes or until mix passes toothpick test.

Let cool ten minutes then cut into squares, sprinkle sugar over squares and add ice cream.

Beer to serve: Ale, bock, porter, stout

Chocolate Cake

Recommended beer: *Porter or stout*

2 oz. unsweetened chocolate

Preheat oven to 350 degrees. Grease and flour 2 8″ cake pans.

Melt chocolate in a double boiler over hot water, or in a microwave oven. Set aside to cool.

1²/₃ c. flour
¼ tsp salt
1½ tsp baking powder
¼ tsp baking soda

Sift together dry ingredients. Set aside.

½ c. shortening
1 c. sugar
2 eggs

Cream the shortening. Gradually beat in the sugar, mixing until light and fluffy. Add eggs, one at a time, beating well after each addition. Stir in the cooled chocolate.

¾ c. beer

Add the dry ingredients alternately with the beer, beating well after each addition.

Pour batter into prepared cake pans. Bake about 25 minutes, or until a toothpick inserted into the center of the pan comes out clean and dry. Cool on a wire rack for about 10 minutes, then remove from pans and cool completely.

Put layers together with lightly sweetened whipped cream.

Beer to serve: Stout, lambic beer

Molasses Cake

Recommended beer: *Porter, sweet stout, barley wine*

1 c. butter
1 c. sugar
1 c. molasses
3 eggs
4 c. flour
1 tsp baking soda
1 tsp salt
1 c. beer

Grease and flour three 8x1½ in. round baking pans. Cream butter and sugar in bowl, add molasses and beat. Add eggs, one at a time, and continue beating.

Pour flour, baking soda and salt into separate bowl and mix. Add into molasses bowl and begin pouring in beer while stirring.

Pour batter into each pan and bake 15 minutes at 375 degrees or until passes toothpick test.

Remove from oven and let cool on wire racks.

2 15-ounce jars chunky
**   applesauce**
½ tsp cinnamon
whipped cream or dessert topping

Clean baking pans, grease and flour again; fill with remaining batter and bake.

Mix cinnamon and applesauce and place on layers of cooled cake. Top with whipped cream or dessert topping.

Beer to serve: Porter, stout, barley wine

Butterscotch pudding

Recommended beer: *Ale, bock, seasonal beer*

1 package butterscotch pudding
2/3 c. nonfat dry milk
1 tsp. pumpkin pie spice
1 c. beer
1 c. water

Combine dry ingredients in saucepan. Pour in beer and water and heat until mixture starts to boil.

Pour into serving bowls, let cool, then chill in refrigerator.

Whipped cream or dessert topping

When pudding has set, remove, top with whipped cream and serve.

Beer to serve: Pale ale, bock, seasonal beer

Tapioca Pudding

Recommended beer: *Amber lager, pale ale*

2 eggs
1½ c. milk
½ c. sugar
¼ c. tapioca
¼ tsp nutmeg
⅛ tsp salt

Beat eggs in saucepan and add milk, sugar, tapioca, nutmeg and salt. Set aside ten minutes.

1 bottle beer
½ c. raisins

Cook tapioca over low heat, stirring. Add beer slowly while stirring. Add raisins, raise heat until almost a boil.

Remove from stove and pour into serving bowls.

Beer to serve: Ale, porter, barley wine

SUGGESTED MENUS

Seasonal menus are fun and easy to prepare. The following menus offer exciting possibilities for the adventurous menu planner hoping to introduce guests to some traditional as well as newly discovered foods that feature specialty beers.

All menus should be accompanied by at least three or four beer styles.

SPRING

Tossed Salad with Beer Dressing
Chopped Liver Spread with Beer and Herbs
Chicken in Beer
Herb Bread
Gingerbread Cake

Spicy Shrimp Salad
Beer-Glazed Ham
Cheddar Muffins
Cole Slaw with Beer Dressing
Fresh Fruit with Beer Custard Sauce

SUMMER

Beer Cheese and Crackers
Barbecued Chicken
Potato Salad
Skillet or Herb Bread
Chocolate Cake with Whipped Cream and Toasted Almonds

Clam and Parmesan Appetizers
Grilled Spiced Pork Chops
Whole Wheat Rolls
Hot German Potato Salad
Apple Pie with Beer Custard Sauce

FALL

Beer Cheese Dip with Fresh Vegetables
Chili
Southwest Salad
Rye Bread
Gingerbread Cake

Spicy Shrimp Salad
Beer Marinated Steak
Baked Potatoes
Whole Wheat Rolls
Brown Sugar Cake

WINTER

Hot Crabmeat Appetizer
Carbonnade a la Flammande
Beer Bread
Chocolate Cake with Hot Cherry Sauce

Beer Batter Onion Rings
Spicy Shrimp
Hearty Chili
Rye Bread
Cheese, Fruit, Pastry Platter

A Last Word

By writing this book I hope I have made a contribution to the literature on the field of cooking with beer.

It still is a mystery to me that, with its abundant properties as a food, its fascinating history and continuing popularity around the world, beer still is largely absent from kitchens. That's a shame. I hope that situation changes so that more amateur and professional cooks will discover the delights and rewards of cooking with this rich and diverse food.

The next few years should find newspapers and magazines devoting more attention to specialty beers as interest in them grows and consumers discover them and the many foods prepared with them. A brewing trade association predicts that the 1990s will be "The Decade of Beer" as specialty imported beers find wider acceptance and microbreweries expand and prosper. I find no reason to dispute that claim and believe that beer ultimately will gain the respectability it richly deserves.

As I do beer dinners around the country I plan to write a brewpub cookbook with recipes developed by the brewmasters and cooks in brewpubs across the U.S. and Canada. Along the way I hope to meet readers and find out what they think about specialty beers and cooking with them.

I hope you'll take time to write and let me know what you think of the recipes, menus and information included in this book. If you have your own favorite recipes, please send them along so I can test and consider them for dinners or articles.

Cheers! Enjoy cooking with specialty beers — I know you will.

Reston, Virginia
July, 1989

Royal Oak Pale Ale
Eldridge Pope Brewery
Dorchester, England

BIBLIOGRAPHY

Although there are countless books on cooking with wine, the literature on cooking with beer is meager. A simple, but probably inaccurate assessment, may have something to do with the experience of Prohibition in America and the somewhat unfortunate reputation beer has had as a "common" or socially inferior beverage. Whatever the reasons, it is unfortunate that there are not more books to turn to for those with an interest in the topic.

Many cookbooks have a token recipe that includes beer, but those are usually for the traditional shrimp batter, stew with ale, or marinade. Interestingly, many of these recipes are from Europe where beer has had a better reputation. In time, the North American cuisine may reflect what European cooks have known for centuries.

SELECTIVE LIST OF BOOKS
THAT USE BEER IN COOKING

Ackart, Robert. "Spirited Cooking: An Introduction to Wines in the Kitchen." New York: Atheneum, 1984. Although there are scant mentions of beer, a Belgian Beer Waffles recipe is tantalizing.

Anderson, Will. "Beer USA." Dobbs Ferry: Morgan & Morgan, 1986. A collection of photos and anecdotes about the influence of beer in American history and culture. Makes for fascinating browsing for anyone curious about the social impact of beer.

Brown, Cora, Rose and Bob. "Cooking with Wine." New York: Castle Books, 1960. Primarily a collection of hundreds of recipes using wine, champagne, and liqueurs. Contains traditional European recipes with beer: Danish Roast Beef with beer, baked smoked herring, Belgian goulash, beef Prussian style.

Culinary Arts Institute. "Cooking with Beer." New York: Dalair Publishing, 1980. One of the more interesting collections of recipes and menus, particularly for desserts and theme parties.

Dickens, Cedric. "Drinking with Dickens." New York: Amsterdam, 1988. First published in Britain in 1980. Cedric presents recipes and anecdotes from his Great-grandfather's novels. He claims that the reason no beer was found in Charles Dickens' cellar after his death was because the servants probably continued to take their daily ration from the pantry supply which never made it all the way to the cellar. He relates a quaint ritual from his Cambridge days of tapping kegs of amber ale, but only after it had been cooled with damp cloths and beds of mustard seed and cress to keep the ale cool before tapping.

Erickson, Jack. "Star Spangled Beer: A Guide to America's New Micro-breweries and Brewpubs." Reston, Virginia: RedBrick Press, 1987. A history and directory of American and Canadian microbreweries including beer styles brewed by each brewery.

Fahy, Carole. "Cooking with Beer." New York: Dover, 1978. This edition is an unabridged republication of a book published in England in 1972. A comprehensive treatment of hundreds of recipes, many with English or continental beers and ales. The only thing lacking in this American edition is information on the influence of the 1972 book.

Finch, Christopher. "Beer: A Connoisseur's Guide to the World's Best." New York: Abbeyville Press, 1989. Although the book's concentration is on specialty beers from around the world, there are many colorful pictures of platters of foods and beers. A beautifully designed and written book; a major addition to the literature of beer.

Gastineau, Clifford, Editor. "Fermented Food Beverages in Nutrition." New York: Academic Press, 1979. A collection of academic papers on alcohol, nutrition, and health.

Jackson, Michael. "Pocket Guide to Beer." Simon & Schuster: New York, 1987. An invaluable resource for the traveler or connoisseur sampling beers from around the world. Precise capsule reports on hundreds of breweries and specialty beers from the international expert.

Harrison, Michael. "Beer Cookery: 101 Traditional Recipes." London: Neville Spearman Ltd. and John Calder Ltd., 1953. A treasure of a book complete with national dishes and an assortment of unusual recipes including Cod Prince Henry the Navigator, beer bangers, bubble and squeak, Bachelor's Repeal Steak, hot beer pudding, beans and beer, and lambswool.

Hewett, Edward and Axton, W.F. "Convivial Dickens: The Drinks of Dickens and His Times." Athens, Ohio: Ohio University Press, 1983. A delightful treatment of literature, history and food and drink during the Victorian era. Includes recipes for drinks other than ale and beer and wonderful drawings from books and articles published by Dickens. One appendix includes the auction catalogue listing the contents from Dickens' cellar at the time of his death, which included 185 dozen bottles of wines, spirits, whiskeys, and champagne. The auction in August, 1870 raised 521 pounds, 17 shillings and sixpence.

Jackson, Michael. "The New World Guide to Beer." Philadelphia: Running Press, 1988. Fully updated from the classic 1977 edition. Jackson has been writing about the benefits of matching beers and food for more than a decade. The book is encyclopedic and filled with notes and comments about foods and specialty beers throughout.

Krajeski, Anita, Editor. "Coors Taste of the West." Des Moines: Meredith Publishing, Second Edition, 1985. A Western theme throughout the book with anecdotes and background notes on saloons, rodeos, barbed wire, Boot Hill, and "sodbuster" pioneers who broke the first ground to build farms in the West. Many creative recipes for game, fish, barbecue, and Mexican dishes. Includes unusual treats such as cactus salad, Indian cookies, chess pie, and "Bowl of the Wife of Kit Carson." A fun, browsing book.

Orton, Vrest. "The Homemade Beer Book." Rutland, VT: Charles E. Tuttle Company, 1973. A reprint of a book first privately published (300 copies) during Prohibition in 1932 and entitled, "Proceedings of the Company of Amateur Brewers." Primarily a book of recipes for traditional homebrews (including George Washington's recipe for "small beer"), the book reveals how creative early brewers were in making exotic ginger beers, spruce beers, "treacle" (made with molasses) and even beer wine! (Actually, wine made from raisins or peaches but fermented with yeast after it has fermented beer.)

Porter, John. "All About Beer." Garden City, New York: Doubleday & Company, 1975. A primer about beer from early history to beer trivia. Includes easy and traditional beer recipes such as cheese and beer souffle, steamed frankfurters with sauerkraut and beef stew with ale.

Root, Waverley & de Rochemont, Richard. "Eating in America." New York: The Ecco Press, 1981. A fascinating and comprehensive account of the role of food in American history, including a long chapter on "Drinking in America."

———. "Official Budweiser Cookbook." Milwaukee, Wisconsin: Ideals Publishing Corp., 1983. Collection of recipes from snacks and light meals to holiday dishes, roasts and casseroles prepared with beer. Includes 9 recipes for chili made with beer.

Waldo, Myra. "Beer and Good Food." Garden City, NY: Doubleday & Co., 1958. Although quite dated, Ms. Waldo's book includes imaginative recipes even though she treats beer as if it were all pale pilsener.

FOOTNOTES

Introduction
1. "All About Beer," John Porter, Doubleday & Co.: Garden City, N.Y., 1975. p. 6.
2. "Cooking with Beer," Carole Fahy, Dover Publications: New York, 1978. p. ix.

Chapter 1
1. "Expedition," Journal of the Museum of Archeology/Anthropology, March 1987. University of Pennsylvania, Dr. Solomon Katz.
2. New York Times, March 24, 1987.
3. New York Times, Jan. 5, 1988. p. C1.
4. "Beer USA," Will Anderson, Morgan & Morgan, Dobbs Ferry, NY. p. 43.
5. "Pocket Guide to Beer," Michael Jackson, Simon & Schuster, 1987. p. 4.

Chapter 7
1. "Convivial Dickens," Hewett, Edward and Axton, W.F. Ohio University Press, Athens, Ohio, 1983. p. 8.
2. ibid. p. 17.

INDEX

Yes, I would like to order the following books from RedBrick Press.

"Star Spangled Beer: A Guide to America's
New Microbreweries and Brewpubs"   0-941397-00-9 $13.95 _____

"Great Cooking With Beer"   0-941397-02-5 $16.95 (Hardcover) _____

0-941397-01-7 $10.95 (Paperback) _____

TAX (Va. 4½%) _____

SHIPPING ($1.50/book) _____

TOTAL _____

RedBrick Press is producing videotapes featuring specialty beers and cooking. To receive information about the videos, please fill out card and mail to RedBrick Press.
☐ **Please send information on specialty beers videos.**

NAME _____

ADDRESS _____

CITY _____ **STATE/PROVINCE** _____ **ZIP** _____

Please send form and check or money order to:

RedBrick Press
P.O. Box 2184
Reston, VA 22090

Yes, I would like to order the following books from RedBrick Press.

"Star Spangled Beer: A Guide to America's
New Microbreweries and Brewpubs"   0-941397-00-9 $13.95 _____

"Great Cooking With Beer"   0-941397-02-5 $16.95 (Hardcover) _____

0-941397-01-7 $10.95 (Paperback) _____

TAX (Va. 4½%) _____

SHIPPING ($1.50/book) _____

TOTAL _____

RedBrick Press is producing videotapes featuring specialty beers and cooking. To receive information about the videos, please fill out card and mail to RedBrick Press.
☐ **Please send information on specialty beers videos.**

NAME _____

ADDRESS _____

CITY _____ **STATE/PROVINCE** _____ **ZIP** _____

Please send form and check or money order to:

RedBrick Press
P.O. Box 2184
Reston, VA 22090